THE CATHOLIC UNIVERSITY OF AMERICA
CANON LAW STUDIES
No. 312

THE JUDICIAL NOTARY

A HISTORICAL SYNOPSIS AND A COMMENTARY

A DISSERTATION

SUBMITTED TO THE FACULTY OF THE SCHOOL OF CANON LAW OF THE CATHOLIC UNIVERSITY OF AMERICA IN PARTIAL FULFILLMENT OF THE REQUIREMENTS FOR THE DEGREE OF DOCTOR OF CANON LAW

BY

REVEREND CHARLES J. DUERR, B.A., J.C.L.

PRIEST OF THE DIOCESE OF GREEN BAY

THE CATHOLIC UNIVERSITY OF AMERICA PRESS
WASHINGTON, D. C.
1951

Nihil Obstat:

DIONYSIUS M. BURKE, O. PRAEM., S.T.D., J.C.D.
Censor Deputatus
Sinus Viridis, die 8 decembris, 1950.

Imprimatur:

STANISLAUS V. BONA, S.T.D., D.D.
Episcopus Sinus Viridis
Sinus Viridis, die 8 decembris, 1950.

MURRAY & HEISTER, INC.
WASHINGTON, D. C.

TO

MY FATHER AND MOTHER

Peter Aloysius Duerr
and
Albertine Haevers Duerr

TABLE OF CONTENTS

FOREWORD

This study is concerned with and limited to that notary who is employed as actuary in ecclesiastical judicial processes. No attempt has been made in the historical synopsis or in the canonical commentary to give a description of the entire notarial system. The study deals with notaries in general only in so far as legislation concerning them affects as well the notary employed as actuary in ecclesiastical judicial processes.

To obviate any difficulties contingent on the use of names, the term "judicial notary" has been used as the standard expression to denote the person employed as clerk of court in ecclesiastical trials. It was felt that to refer to him simply as notary would be perhaps misleading, since that term has a wider connotation. To call him the chancellor, a term sometimes used by the authors and found in the sources, would be ambiguous in view of the present day usage of that term. And so with the other terms.

The Code of Canon Law did little to standardize this notary employed as actuary. The Instructions of the Sacred Congregations also have been seemingly reluctant to settle on one term. While "judicial notary" *(notarius iudicialis)* may not become the accepted standard expression, it is sincerely submitted that it will prove an aid to standardization.

The historical synopsis which forms the first section of this study is just that—a synopsis, and no claim is laid to the presentation of a full history. On the other hand, the history has not been relegated to a minor position. Both the historical synopsis and the canonical commentary make up the full picture of the office of the judicial notary as it functions today. To understand the present legislation on the office of the judicial notary a grasp of the historical background is essential.

The procedural law of the Code connotes a wide field of action in law. The norms for the various types of processes have been set up by the Code. The Code demands a notary to be employed as recorder for every process. To delineate the role of the judicial notary in every trial, point by point, would take up several studies. And it would be repetitious work. The office and the functions and the rights of the judicial notary are practically uniform in every process. In view of this fact, the attempt has been made to give general, over-all descriptions of the nature of the office and the duties of the judicial notary in as practical and serviceable a manner as possible. Of course, since the judicial notary is so closely connected with judicial acts, each act could conceivably have been analyzed in its relation to the judicial notary. Such procedure, it is felt, would only labor the obvious.

The subject matter of this study is only the notary employed in judicial procedure. It is not a study of the canonical procedural law, or of judicial acts, or of special types of processes, or of the diocesan tribunal or even of the eccesiastical notarial system. The main purpose is to delineate solely the office of the judicial notary. No particular judicial process will be detailed. The roles of the other officials of the court have been treated in other studies. There is no intention to repeat here a detailed description of these roles inasmuch as they are related in some manner or fashion to that of the judicial notary.

Finally, while the theoretical aspects have not been neglected, emphasis has been placed on the practical points. Upon the previous fixation and discussion of the general norms of law, some of the more salient points have been treated as illustrative material. Perhaps to some this study will seem somewhat sketchy. It is not meant to be such. The object has been to cover only one subject in a manner complete and interesting indeed, but withal concise. If that has been done satisfactorily, it is due to the kind help and unfailing assistance of all the members of the Faculty of the School of Canon Law at The Catholic University of America.

The Most Reverend Stanislaus V. Bona, D.D., Bishop of Green Bay, graciously afforded the writer the opportunity to pursue the course of graduate studies in Canon Law and constantly encouraged him therein. The writer welcomes this occasion to express his sincere gratitude to Bishop Bona.

During the years of study, the Rev. Peter A. Duerr, the writer's brother, was always ready with willing support. The Rev. Basil R.

Reuss, O. Praem., professor at Saint Norbert's College, and the Very Rev. Dr. Gregory J. Roettger, O.S.B., J.U.D., professor of Canon Law at Saint John's Seminary, have been constant sources of knowledge and inspiration during and after college and seminary years. The Very Rev. Dr. Dennis M. Burke, O. Praem., S.T.D., J.C.D., kindly read over the manuscript and offered many helpful suggestions. The writer will always be truly grateful to them and to the many others who in any way assisted during the years of study.

CHAPTER I

THE JUDICIAL NOTARY IN THE EARLY CHURCH

Article 1. Preliminary Remarks

The Church as a perfectly sovereign society instituted by Jesus Christ is endowed with judicial power.[1] In the years immediately following the institution of the Church there is little evidence to show that this power was exercised. For example, the members of the Church at Corinth in the middle of the first century were the object of concern to the "Apostle of the Gentiles," Paul, in this regard. Saint Paul discovered certain abuses in regard to civil litigation. It was, in part, the purpose of Saint Paul in writing to the Church at Corinth to correct abuses that existed in the ecclesiastical judicial order. Writing ca. 57, Saint Paul rebuked the Corinthians: "Dare any of you, having a matter against another, bring your case to be judged before the unjust and not before the saints?"[2]

Reference is clearly made to ecclesiastical courts. Unfortunately there are not any records of the procedure, nor was there any mention of a person who served in the capacity of court notary. From its beginning, however, the Church knew judicial action.[3]

An unhistorical tradition contained in the *Liber Pontificalis* relates that Pope Clement I (ca. 88-97) divided the Church at Rome into seven regions, and that in these regions he appointed notaries who were to compile accurate and diligent accounts of the acts of the martyrs.[4] In order to know who these notaries were and what other duties they had, it is necessary to look to the legal systems

---

[1] Ottaviani, *Compendium Iuris Publici Ecclesiastici* (Typis Polyglottis Vaticanis, 1936), nn. 85-88, pp. 170-178.

[2] I Cor., VI:1.

[3] Cf. such Scriptural texts as I Tim., V:19; Matt., XVIII:15-18.

[4] "Hic [Clemens I] fecit VII regiones, dividit notariis fidelibus ecclesiae, qui gestas martyrum sollicite et curiose unusquisque per regionem suam, diligenter perquireret"—Duchesne, *Le Liber Pontificalis* (2 vols., 1886-1892, Vol. I, Paris, 1886), I n. IV, 1.2, p. 123 (hereafter cited *Liber Pontificalis*).

existing in the early centuries of the Church's history. Since this study is concerned with the person who was employed in the ecclesiastical judicial system as clerk of the court, it is necessary first of all to outline in general terms the notarial system from whose ranks he was taken. The attempt will be made to delineate the office of the judicial notary in particular. The Roman law system must be examined first of all, however, for evidence of the early notary employed as actuary—the judicial notary.

Article 2. The Judicial Notary in the Roman Law System

A. The Church and Roman Law

The use of terms presents formidable problems in regard to the history of the judicial notary. The Roman law, to which the Church fell heir,[5] used various terms to indicate the forerunner of the ecclesiastical judicial notary. In the seventh century the Church adopted, as the letters of Pope Gregory the Great indicate, the Roman law *de judiciis*.[6] But Roman law was not slavishly adopted. Rather, canonical procedure was the result of the fusion of Roman law elements in great part with the Germanic law, with statutes and customs, and with the institutes which the Church itself established.[7] The office of the ecclesiastical court notary has its roots in Roman law. The notary's presence at court in ecclesiastical trials was first required by the legislation of the IV General Council of the Lateran (1215), but this does not mean that notaries were not employed in the courts before that time.[8]

B. The Roman Scriba

The problem of discovering just who was and what was the judicial notary, and of gauging his relation to the notariate in Roman law, is made complicated through the confusing use of terms which served to indicate such a court employee. During the Republic and

[5] Roberti, *De Processibus* (2 vols., Vol. I, 2. ed, Romae: Apud Custodiam Librariam Pontificii Instituti Utriusque Iuris, 1941), I, n. 2.

[6] Roberti, *loc. cit.*

[7] Roberti, *ibid.*, p. 3.

[8] Mansi, *Sacrorum Conciliorum Nova et Amplissima Collectio* (53 vols. in 60, Paris-Leipzig-Arnhem, 1901-1937), XXII, 1023-1026 (hereafter cited Mansi).

down to the age of the great jurisconsults (Early Empire) *scriba* was the name generally given to those who copied public acts.[9] In the classical period and in the time of the early jurists, *scriba* was the general term for a clerk of the court, though it often was used for anyone professing the act of writing.[10] The concept of *scriba* contains the idea of *notarius*. Paul Fournier (1855-1935) described the notary as being a scribe in the more general sense of that term.[11]

It seems accordingly that the judicial notary was in the early stage of his history known as the *scriba*. Moreover, "originally a *notarius* was a writer, probably associated with the *scriba*, who took down material for deeds in the form of *notae*, using what in effect was a system of shorthand."[12]

C. *The Roman* EXCEPTOR

In the fourth and fifth centuries (the Later Empire) the language changed completely. The judicial notary was then known as the *exceptor*. It was the *exceptor* who performed the duties, such as they were, of the clerk of the court, while *notarii* were the secretaries of the emperor.[13] Earlier than the fourth century the *exceptor* was universally understood to be a private copier. It was in the fourth and fifth centuries, however, that the term became recognized as the general term for a clerk of the court.[14] The *Notitia dignitatum* shows that *exceptores* were attached to all governmental bureaus.[15] The copyists of the courts bear the same name.[16]

According to a Constitution of Emperor Honorius (395-423) in 396, in the legal proceedings before the curia of a city one magis-

---

[9] D. (50. 4) (18. 17): ". . . scribae magistratus personali munere serviunt."

[10] Brown, "The Origin and Early History of the Office of Notary," *The Juridical Review* (Edinburgh: Green and Son, 1888——), XLVII (1935), n. 3, p. 209 (hereafter cited Brown).

[11] *Les Officialites au Moyen Age* (Paris: E. Plon, 1880), p. 11.

[12] Brown, p. 210.

[13] Savigny, *Geschichte des romischen Rechts im Mittelalter* (2 ed., 7 vols., Heidelberg, 1834-1851), I, n. 16 (hereafter cited Savigny).

[14] Brown, p. 213.

[15] *Codex Theodosianus,* (8.7) 17; *Codex Iustinianus,* (12. 49 [50]) 5. Mention of an *actuarius* is made, but in employment other than in the courts: *Codex Iustinianus,* (12. 49 [50]) 6.

[16] *Codex Iustinianus,* (12. 19) (12. 1).

trate, three principals, and the *exceptor* were required to be present.[17] The non-mention of these in the Justinian Code[18] was pointed out by Savigny (1779-1861) as almost certainly explained in the fact that their presence was tacitly implied.[19] From the foregoing it appears that the presence of a notary in court, known as an *exceptor*, was part of the Roman law system.[20]

D. *The Roman* TABELLIO *and* NOTARIUS

In Roman law there was mention also of the *tabellio*. Although he could be mistaken for the judicial or the court notary, he was the forerunner rather of the modern notary public than of the clerk of the court. These *tabelliones* were persons who, without being public officers, drew up transactions, wills, etc.[21] The *tabellio* was in reality a person who drew up contracts and other instruments of private interests. Without a doubt the ministry of these *tabelliones* was not required, for Roman law took into consideration also other writings, although the use of a *tabellio* was of an advantageous character in connection with the drawing up of documents.[22]

The term *notarius* may at first glance appear to be equivalent in meaning to the term "notary," in the sense namely that only a *notarius* was a notary. Yet, to identify the *notarius* or notary exclusively with the *tabellio* would be erroneous. The *tabellio*, often simply referred to as a notary and later identified with that term, was the equivalent of our modern notary public.[23] He was the notary spoken of in the forty-fourth and seventy-seventh *Novellae* of Justinian (527-565). In the course of time "this original distinction between *notarius* and *tabellio* gradually disappeared, and *notarius* became the general term as among the Lombards, where it would seem that

[17] *Codex Theodosianus*, (12. 1) 151.

[18] *Codex Iustinianus*, (1. 56) 2.

[19] Savigny, I, n. 96.

[20] In support of this is the *Digest*, (4.6) 33: ". . . eos qui notis scribunt acta praesidum rei publicae causa non abesse certum est"; and *Novellae* 47 (17.4): ". . . unde sancimus et eos quicumque gestis ministrant, sive in iudiciis sive ubicumque conficiuntur acta . . ."

[21] Savigny, I, n. 16.

[22] P. Fournier, *Les Officialites au Moyen Age*, p. 11.

[23] Brown, p. 218; Savigny, *loc. cit.*

the two terms first commenced to be synonymous."[24] In the sixth century, *amanuenses* and *cancellarii* were other terms used in designation of the *tabelliones*.[25]

Laborderie-Boulou described the *notarius* as being in his early history a slave who took down the notes of his master. Sometimes he was a freedman. The Roman practice knew also the *servi publici* who were charged with transcribing the acts of the magistrates. Moreover, "a la fin des temps classiques, peut-etre des Aurelien, les empereurs eurent leurs *notarii*. Les prefets du pretoire eurent egalement leurs *notarii* repandu dans tous leurs bureaux: ce furent les *exceptores*. Remarquons, d'ailleurs, que *servi publici, notarii, exceptores* se raprochent plus du greffier moderne que du notarie." [26]

The *tabellio* was indeed the ancestor of the modern notary. "The Digest and Code of Justinian revealed to the medieval civilians a state of society where special agents prepared documents. From the Roman law texts the famous Italian founder of the Bologna school of the Glossators, Irnerius, derived and introduced the modern conception of a notary."[27]

ARTICLE 3. THE NOTARIAL SYSTEM IN THE EARLY CHURCH

In the first three centuries the Church at Rome had essentially no organization different from that which prevailed in the churches of the sees of other bishops. In a privileged category belonged the notaries whose task it was to write the acts of the martyrs, and who attended to the official correspondence and office work of the Papal See.

The reputed fact of the establishment of seven regional notaries to record the acts of the martyrs has been recorded above. More evidence is added in regard to this use of notaries in the reign of

---

[24] Brown, p. 363, note 4.

[25] *Codex Theodosianus*, (9.19) 1.

[26] Laborderie-Boulou, "Recherches sur les Origines de la Responsabilite Notariale," *Revue Generale du Droit* (Paris, 1876——), XXXVI (1912), p. 386, note 1.

[27] Sherman, *Roman Law in the Modern World* (2. ed., 3 vols., New York: Baker, Voorhis & Co., 1924), II, 458.

Pope Anteros (235-236).[28] In the reign of the succeeding Supreme Pontiff, Fabianus (236-250), seven subdeacons were appointed in charge over these *notarii.* Since these notaries used *notae,* an abbreviated form of writing, the subdeacons were further instructed to write out the *acta* in full, and to preserve the complete records.[29] In the fourth century a special use of notaries was established. Julius I (337-352) decreed that clerics were to have their legal difficulties settled in ecclestiastical courts. The *primicerius notariorum* was to publish *omnia monumenta;* the *notitia* was to be collected by the *notarii.*[30]

After the time of Emperor Constantine (+ 337) the notaries of the holy Roman Church are sufficiently attested. They formed a *schola* or guild, just as the notaries did at the imperial court. Evidence from Roman law indicate that the Roman law notaries were organized into a corporation.[31] In the Roman law system their chief duties were the preparation of the legal documents,[32] the framing of the *libelli* or the complaints for the commencement of lawsuits,[33] and the drafting of wills.[34]

In the Church, the *schola* was made up of the seven *notarii regionarii.* The chief of the *schola* was known as the *primicerius notariorum.* He was a counsellor of the Pope, and was entrusted with the discharge of the official business. This came with the elaboration of the papal court, especially commencing with Pope Damasus (366-384), when there were introduced certain palace officials, among whom were those known as the *iudices palatini.* These play-

---

[28] "Hic [Anteros] gestas martyrum diligenter a notariis exquisivit et in ecclesia recondit . . ."—Duchesne, *Liber Pontificalis,* I, 147.

[29] "Hic regiones dividit diaconibus et fecit VII subdiaconos qui VII notariis inminerent, ut gestas martyrum in integro fideliter colligerent, et multas fabricas per cymeteria fieri praecepit."—Duchesne, *Liber Pontificalis,* I, 148. In the *notes explicatives* Duchesne indicated that *inminere* has here the same meaning as in the letters of Saint Gregory, where it signifies "to guard," that is, to insure that such a person does what he ought to do.

[30] Duchesne, *Liber Pontificalis,* I, 205.

[31] *Codex Iustinianus,* (10.71) (1.1).

[32] *Codex Iustinianus,* (4.21) (17.2).

[33] D. (48.19) (9. 4-7).

[34] *Codex Iustinianus,* (6.22), (8.1-2).

ed a conspicuous part in the period between the fourth and the twelfth centuries.[35]

At the head of the college or the *schola* was the *primicerius*, the chief keeper of the archives. He was one of three officials who ruled the Roman Church in the absence of the Pope. The other two were the archdeacon and the archpresbyter.[36] Sometimes he was a married man.[37]

The *scrinium* was the office of the notaries, the chancery. As early as the time of Gregory the Great (590-604) the *notarii* were also known as *scriniarii*. The notarial system before the time of Pope Adrian I (772-795) was composed of six officers. Not all the principals were, either in fact or of necessity, notaries, although they formed what was called the college of notaries, and the office was called the *scrinium*. The *primicerius* was aided by the *secundicerius*. The treasurer, or the keeper of the chest, was known as the *arcarius*. The Pope's paymaster, in the seventh century, went by the name of *saccellarius*. The modern social worker would find his historical prototype in the *primicerius defensorum*. The *nomenclator* or *amminiculator* appeared in 678-681, chiefly to receive and deal with petitions that were presented to the Pope during processions. The seventh officer was the *protoscriniarius*, sometimes referred to as the *protus*. He did not appear before the year 861.[38] He was not usually a member of the college. He was the head of the *tabelliones* or public scriveners who drew up deeds for private persons.[39]

All of these department heads usually belonged to the clergy, though they generally were in Minor Orders only. There is much more evidence for the role of notaries in papal administration. Only the briefest outline has been presented here to give the background of the judicial notary, his family background, so to speak.

There is some evidence to indicate the use of notaries in judicial

---

[35] Hilling, *Procedure at the Roman Curia* (New York: Wagner, 1907), p. 12.

[36] Roziere, *Liber Diurnus* (Paris, 1869), p. 108, n. 59.

[37] Poole, *Lectures on the History of the Papal Chancery* (Cambridge: Cambridge Press, 1915), p. 17.

[38] Poole, *ibid.*, p. 19.

[39] *Ibid.*, p. 52.

matters. During the reign of Gregory the Great (590-604), when the *schola* of notaries was flourishing, this pope sent John, "*notarius sedis nostrae*," to investigate the accusations made against an archbishop in Sardinia, and to call upon the archbishop to prove his innocence, if that he could do, by producing documents that would clear him of the charges.[40]

Earlier than this, Pope Hormisdas (514-523) sent a certain Hilary, a notary, on a mission to Greece along with two bishops, a priest and a deacon.[41] The use that Pope Gregory made of some notaries, however, indicates the judicial order. In another case, a notary by the name of Pantaleon was sent by him to investigate a charge of rape that had been called to his attention because of the personages involved. Pantaleon was sent to conduct a trial, or at least an investigation. If the accused was found guilty, the notary was instructed to enforce his contracting of marriage, or, if the culprit refused, he was to be beaten and then sent to a monastery to do penance.[42]

From the time of Charlemagne onward the office of notary gradually rose to such a status that it was frequently exercised by deacons and priests.[43]

An interesting document that concerned procedure outside the papal chancery was the letter of Hincmar, the celebrated archbishop of Rheims (845-882), written in 882. In this letter Hincmar mentioned the *apocrisiarius* as ruling the clerics of the *palatium*, the *cancellarius* who took care of writing and preserving the documents, and the *comes palatii* who was appointed ". . . *ut omnes contentiones legales . . . iuste et rationabiliter determinaret* . . ."[44] Concerning the latter, "*comes palatii de omnibus saecularibus causis vel iudiciis suscipiendi curam instanter habebat.*"[45]

---

[40] Thomassinus, *Vetus et Nova Ecclesiae Disciplina circa Beneficia et Beneficiarios* (10 vols., *Magontiaci*, 1787), Pars I, lib II, c. 104, n. 8 (hereafter cited Thomassinus).

[41] Duchesne, *Liber Pontificalis*, I, 269.

[42] Thomassinus, Pars. I, lib. II, c. 104, n. 8.

[43] Thomassinus, *loc. cit.*

[44] Hincmarus, *De Ordine Palatii*, (edidit Victor Krause, Hannoverae et Lipsiae, 1894), c. 21, p. 17.

[45] *Ibid.*, c. 19, p. 16.

ARTICLE 4. THE PERSONAL STATUS OF THE NOTARY

What was the personal status of these notaries? According to the opinion of Thomassinus (1619-1695), lay notaries were rare, since laymen were not considered to be as trustworthy as clerics, even apart from the general condition that in comparison with clerics they likewies were "*rudes*."[46]

In every Christian church from primitive times onward the use of writing served a beneficial purpose. It was necessary to copy the holy Bible, liturgical books, letters, acts of the martyrs, canons of councils, etc. All of this required competent workers and specialized offices. There were no fixed or permanent offices in relation to the diocesan curia until the fourth century. In the beginning the bishop had complete immediate charge of his diocese. The clergy, the faithful, and all church property were under his direct control. If there was need of any special help, the bishop could appoint a particular cleric for the performance of the duty. The office was discontinued when the work was completed.[47]

What was the position of the notary in regard to the power of Orders in the Church? Did the notariate constitute one of the Minor Orders? Ennodius, Bishop of Pavia (513-521), wrote that Epiphanius, Bishop of Pavia from 466-497, undertook the office of lector when he was eight years old, and became a *notarius* at the age of sixteen.[48]

An important piece of evidence in reference to the question of what role the notariate played in the preparation for the reception of scared or Major Orders is furnished by a document of Pope Gelasius (492-496), written in 494. Referring to advancement in Orders, Pope Gelasius decreed:

> " . . . ut si quis, etiam de religioso proposito et disciplinis monasterialibus eruditus, ad clericale munus accedit, im-

---

[46] *Vetus et Nova Ecclesiae Disciplina circa Beneficia et Beneficarios*, Pars. I, lib. II, c. 106, n. 3.

[47] Maroto, *Institutiones Iuris Canonici* (2 vols., Vol. II, Romae, 1919), II, n. 760; Dugan, *The Judiciary Department of the Diocesan Curia*, The Catholic University of America Canon Law Studies, n. 26 (Washington, D. C.: The Catholic University of America, 1925,) p. 8.

[48] Thomassinus, Pars I, lib. II, c. 104, n. 1.

> primis eius vita praeteritis acta temporibus inquiratur; . . . si assecutus est letteras, sine quibus vix fortassis ostiarium possit implere: ut si his omnibus quae sunt praedicta fulcitur, continuo lector vel notarius aut certe defensor effectus, post tres menses existat acolythus, maxime si huic aetas etiam suffragatur, sexto mense subdiaconi nomen accipiat . . . nono mense diaconus completoque anno sit presbyter."[49]

If the notariate did not constitute one of the Minor Orders, it had a very close relationship to them. Another point in this regard is furnished through the contents of a letter written by Gregory the Great concerning a subdeacon in Italy. Finding that continency was being more strictly enforced, the subdeacon in question receded from the Order of subdeaconship in order to function again as a notary.[50]

The notariate in the Italian dioceses of Cremona and Lucca in the seventh century did not seem to be more than a state or stage in the preparation for the reception of scared or Major Orders. In support of this it has been claimed that it was an employment, and an office, which could be given even to a cleric constituted in the subdiaconate, or in the priesthood.[51] This interpretation, which regards the notariate as not having been a Minor Order, is however far from certain.

From the late seventh century onward each church had an organized system of notaries integrated in the clerical corps. This was the case at Ravenna, Milan, Cremona, Lucca, Pavia, and of course at Rome, as outlined above. The notarial art, however, was not a

---

[49] Jaffe, *Regesta Pontificum Romanorum ab condita Ecclesia ad annum post Christum natum MCXCVIII* (2. ed., cura G. Wattenbach, F. Kaltenbrunner [ad annum 590], P. Ewald [590-882] and S. Lowenfeld [882-1198], and so cited as JK, JE, JL, 2 vols., Lipsiae, (1885-1888), JK, n. 636; Epistola XIV, c. 2, Thiel, *Epistolae Romanorum Pontificum Genuinae a S. Hilario usque ad II*, Vol. I, *Epistolae Romanorum Pontificum a S. Hilario usque ad S. Hormisdam* (Brunsbergae, 1886), pp. 362-363.

[50] Thomassinus, Pars I, lib. II, c. 104, n. 8.

[51] E. Fournier, "*L'Origine du Vicaire General et des Autres Membres de la Curie Diocesaine* (Paris: Seminaire des Missions Etrangeres, 1940), p. 22 (hereafter cited *L'Origine*).

personal monopoly: anybody who could write was eligible. Official appointment and recognition was another matter.[52]

In the church at Arles, to carry the bishop's *baculum* and to care for it was part of the office of the notary.[53]

The history of the church at Milan has the most to offer in evidence of the liturgical role that the notary played, since Milan is known to have conserved the marks of the primitive notary's existence. There the notary sang the response to the psalms. In 1169 the archbishop confirmed all the privileges of his cathedral church, and included the privileges of the notary.[54] The notarial office was always held in high esteem at Milan.

The description of the Milanese rite by Beroldus delineated the liturgical role of the notary to a greater extent. In the processions, those of the order of notary preceded the lectors and the *clavicularii*. The notary followed closely behind the priests.[55]

In the eighth century the churches of regulars (i.e., of monks) had their own notaries, as did the churches in the control of seculars. The abbeys, as did the other large churches, had their own notaries.[56]

---

[52] E. Fournier, *L'Origine*, pp. 25, 26.

[53] Migne, *Patrologiae Cursus Completus, Series Latina* (221 vols., Parisiis, 1844-1864), LXVII, 1034; Thomassinus, Pars I, lib. II, c. 104, n. 13.

[54] E. Fournier, *L'Origine*, pp. 17-18.

[55] Lejay, "Ambrosien (Rit)"—*Dictionnaire d'Archeologie Chretienne et de Liturgie* (edited by F. Cabrol and H. Leclercq, 14 vols., Paris: Librairie Letouzey et Ane 1907-1939), vol. I (1924), 1392.

[56] E. Fournier, *op. cit.*, p. 31.

CHAPTER II

THE JUDICIAL NOTARY FROM 1215 TO 1545

Artical 1. The Conciliar and Decretal Legislation

With the advent of the thirteenth century the notary made his official appearance in ecclesiastical courts. A decree of the IV General Council of the Lateran (1215) definitely and clearly set up a clerk of the court.[1] The office of the judicial notary was thus set up in the Church in an abiding manner. The development of this office of notary in the courts took place in the years following. The clerk of the court was to be a *persona publica*. In the centuries following its institution, the position of the judicial notary was clearly outlined. The question of what the office was did not require much attention, since the legislation was clear on this point. It was, for the most part, the manner of functioning that was elaborated.

Pope Alexander III (1159-1181) had earlier recognized the value of public acts drawn up by a public person, or by a notary public, and the pope himself attached credence to such documents.[2]

With the increase of the incidence of judicial processes, Pope Innocent III (1198-1216) saw the need of witnesses in attestation of what had gone on during a trial. In the method of court procedure current at that time, the judge was often alone with the person being questioned. The pope had serious misgivings concerning the personal trustworthy character of judges when only one judge was involved in a case, with no one else present except the one being questioned and the judge himself.[3] When a dispute arose as to what had actually transpired in a session, accurate court records were indeed of inestimable value for the settling of the point at issue.

Innocent III regarded notaries rather highly, and he was not slow to defend them against accusations which impugned their trust-

[1] Can. 38—Mansi, XXII, 1023-1026.

[2] C. 2, X, *de fide instrumentorum*, II, 22; JL, n. 13162.

[3] C. 28, X, *de testibus et attestantibus*, II, 20.

worthiness. In one case the allegation was made that a *scriniarius* had falsified the testimony taken by him in a dispute concerning a castle. Innocent was unwilling to believe that a *scriniarius,* since he had sworn to fulfill faithfully his office, would write anything except that which had been said by a witness.[4] Apparently, the use of a recorder in court was not unknown before his employment was required by force of the law.

In view of the situation facing the courts when witness and judge were often alone in gathering testimony and with the number of trials increasing and the judicial procedure developing as a consequence, the logical solution was to appoint a person empowered with making acts authentic in order to record the acts of the court in a competent manner. From whose ranks was such a person to be taken? It was to the notaries, or *tabelliones* as they were called, that Innocent looked. If a notary was not available, two witnesses could fulfill the same task. The presence of this notary was required in every ordinary and extraordinary proceeding. It was the duty of the judge to see to it that a notary was present. All the acts of the case were to be written up. Time, place, and persons were to be noted in the acts.The proceedings were to make up a permanent record, and to be on file for reference if needed. A judge who was negligent in this matter of appointment was liable to punishment.[5]

Thus was established, or rather stabilized, the position of the notary in ecclesiastical trials. Although he had been on hand before in some cases, now his presence demonstrated the employment of a requisite and not simply of an arbitrary factor. This decree of Innocent was embodied in the IV General Council of the Lateran (1215), It was later incorporated in the Decretals of Gregory IX (1227-1241) in 1234.[6]

Because of its importance for the history of the judicial notary, the entire text of this famous legislation is here given:

Since against the false assertion of an unjust judge the innocent party sometimes cannot prove the truth of a denial, because by the

[4] C. 13, X, *De praescriptionibus,* II, 26.

[5] Can. 38 of the IV General Council of the Lateran (1215).

[6] C. 11, X, *de probationibus,* II, 19.

very nature of things there is no direct proof of one denying a fact, that falsity may not prejudice the truth, and injustice may not prevail over justice, we decree that in an ordinary as well as extraordinary inquiry (*iudicium*) let the judge always employ either a public person (if he can be had) or two competent men who shall faithfully take down in writing all the acts of the inquiry, namely, citations and delays, refusals and exceptions, petitions and replies, interrogations and confessions, the depositions of witnesses and presentation of documents, interlocutions, appeals, renunciations, decisions, and other acts which take place must be wirtten down in convenient order, the time, places, and persons to be designated. A copy of everything thus written is to be handed to each of the parties, the originals are to remain in possession of the writers; so that if a dispute should arise in regard to any action of the judge, the truth can be established by a reference to these documents. This provision is made to protect the innocent party against judges who are imprudent and dishonest. A judge who neglects to observe this decree, if on account of this neglect some difficulty should arise, let him be duly punished by a superior judge; nor is there any presumption in favor of doing things his way unless it be evident from legitimate documents in the case.[7]

Article 2. The Rise of the Judicial Notary

As a result of the institution of the judicial notary, and of the legislation which required his presence in a court of law and in judicial proceedings, this notary flourished in the episcopal chanceries. In the period up to 1295 various names were used in indication of the notary who was employed in this manner. He was employed in the archdeacon's court as well as in the episcopal courts. Subscriptions such as the following were appended: "*clericus curie,*" "*clericus juratus curie,*" "*clericus fidelis curie,*" "*mandatus curie,*" "*tabellio curie,*" "*notarius curie.*"[8]

---

[7] Schroeder, *Disciplinary Decrees of the General Councils* (St. Louis: Herder, 1937), pp. 272-273.

[8] P. Fournier, *Les Officialites au Moyen Age*. pp. 46, 47. It is interesting to note the variety of names. There does not seem to be a set formula in the subscriptions that Fournier listed in the documents he cited. Almost without

The organization of a college of judicial notaries at each court was almost a necessary adjunct to the legislation which prescribed their presence in the courts. As their importance increased as also the number of the notaries so employed, it was only natural that regulations should be enacted for the purpose of preserving order among the notaries. Everywhere the judicial notary was expected to take a professional oath before entering on his duties. In certain parts of France examinations on the "*stylus curie*" and on the statutes of the court were required for all candidates to the notariate. Then, too, as a safeguard against possible fraud, the candidate was required to enter his signature in a special register of inscriptions. The acts which were purported as having been recorded by him could thus be checked for their authenticity.[9]

The use of judicial notaries "*per turnum*" was in vogue in some courts. In any case, he was designated by the judge.[10]

It was a frequent occurrence among officials to delegate to a notary all or part of the drawing up of a case, to make the inquiries, and to write up the confession. Such delegation was given in writing. Oftentimes the notary was deputized by the judge to receive the *recognitiones*. Having completed his commission, he drew up a *rescriptum* and sent it to the bishop's court under his seal. When this was read in front of the parties concerned, or of their representatives, it was by this formality that the acts were rendered *in forma publica*. The practice in the north of France did not at first admit of this power of notary to confer on acts the *forma publica*, but this restriction gradually disappeared. Frequently the notary even received the commission to execute decisions, citations, monitions, sentences, etc.[11]

At Autun the judicial notary was required to finish one case before starting another one. No one was allowed to function as notary in two different courts. Moreover, the offices of judicial notary and procurator were regarded as incompatible.[12]

---

exception the official is identified as a cleric. The language was quite fluid and flexible.

[9] P. Fournier, *Les Officialites au Moyen Age*, pp. 53, 54.

[10] P. Fournier, *Les Officialites au Moyen Age*, p. 48.

[11] P. Fournier, *Les Officialites au Moyen Age*, pp. 49-51.

[12] P. Founier, *op. cit.*, 55.

Only a notary was charged to write the acts of a process. He was designated as the "*notarius deputatus ad acta scribenda.*" A special mandate was, at least in theory, necessary for each of the acts which the notary was to admit to the record. This mandate was sometimes given *viva voce.* When the notary was drawing up a confession or the *acta* on his own, it was recommended that he use some circumspection in the matter. If the party was known to him personally, or his identity attested by trustworthy witnesses, so much the better.[13]

The advocate had the obligation to see to it that the acts were accurate. Furthermore, he was to take care that nothing prejudicial to his client which was in any way contrary to the truth was entered in the register of the acts.[14]

Another problem that faced the courts with the introduction of the judicial notary was that of the court records. It seems that in the beginning there were difficulties arising from the transcribing of the testimony and of the acts of the case, namely when different versions of the same court testimony resulted. The mounting confusion and growing abuse were finally suppressed, and order was established through the setting up of court statutes that governed the *registra.* At first the notary had written judicial proceedings on his own register. Such proceedings were the equivalent of the modern "minutes." The needed reform was not long in coming In the reign of Philip the Fair (1285-1314) the royal ordinances marked the introduction of the important reform in France: the processual acts were to be inscribed on special registers *(registra curiae)*, which were to be preserved carefully, and in which the notary was to note when his commission expired.

The *notarius deputatus ad acta scribenda* became a permanent functionary charged with holding the court registers, which were distinct from the notarial. It is not known if that reform which was started in the civil courts was due to similar action in ecclesiastical tribunals, from which the royal jurisdictions had often borrowed in the past. Certainly, at the end of the fourteenth century

[13] P. Fournier, *loc. cit.*

[14] P. Fournier, *Les Officialites au Moyen Age*, p. 49.

the ecclesiastical courts had adopted that regime: they had then the "*notaires-greffiers,*" or clerks of the court.[15]

Article III. Development

Papal power was at a low ebb with the transfer of the seat of the papacy from Rome to Avignon in 1309. It was during the time of the so-called "Babylonian Capitvity" (1309-1376), however, that the development of and progress in the notarial system made great strides. No small part of the credit was due to the personal initiative of one of the greatest administrators of the Avignon popes, John XXII (1316-1334). The development of the central courts cannot be regarded as fully matured before the issuance of the codified regulations of John XXII in 1331. The development of the judicial notary was directly dependent, of course, on the evolution of the judicial system.

At the papal curia, *palatium* was the normal term for the court of law, otherwise known as the *audientia causarum.* The stabilization and consolidation of an already functioning system was effected by these regulations of 1331. This is the earliest known basis of the formation of the Roman Rota.[16]

The use of a notary was specifically required by these regulations. It was his duty to take down in the registers clearly, distinctly and substantially all the acts.[17]

---

[15] P. Fournier, *Les Officialites au Moyen Age,* p. 57.

[16] A number of very competent studies have been made on the history of the Rota. For complete information on the notary, cf. the following: Cerchiari, *Capellani Papae et Apostolicae Sedis, Auditores Causarum Sacri Palatii Apostolici seu S. R. Rotae, ab Origine ad Diem usque 20 sept., 1870* (4 vols., Romae, 1919-1921, I, 116-131; Baumgarten, "Die papstlichen Notare im dreizehnten, vierzehnten und funfzehnten Jahrhundert," *Gorres-Gesellschaft zur Pflege der Wissenschaft im katholischen Deutschland, Veroffentlichungen der Sektion fur Rechts und Staatswissenschaft* (Koln, 1908; Paderborn, 1909-1939), IV-I (1908), 1-68; Schneider, "Der Romische Rota," *Gorres-Gesellschaft zur Pflege der Wissenschaft im katholischen Deutschcland, Veroffentlichungen der Sektion fur Rechts und Staatswissenschaft,* XXII (1914), 132-147.

[17] Ioannes XXII, const. *Ratio iuris,* 16 nov. 1331, n. 26—Tangl, *Die papstlichen Kanzleiordnungen* (Innsbruck, 1894), const. XI, p. 86 (hereafter cited Tangl).

From even a hurried inspection of the Constitution that embodied the regulations it is evident that the appointment of notaries in the *audientia sacrii palatii* was made privately by the auditors themselves. This matter of the appointment in the sense of a designation of the judicial notary is one of the salient features of the legislation regarding notaries For this reason that part of the legislation has been chosen for discussion here. Auditors were not supplied with notaries by the court or the curia as the need arose. In support of this statement can be adduced the regulation that auditors could not make use of the services of a notary who was in the employ of one of the colleagues of the auditor.[18] The notary was to remain with his auditor. The very wording of the regulation shows this close relationship.[19] Furthermore, in the oath of office taken by the notary he had to swear that he would not act either as promotor or as procurator in the suits which were conducted before his auditor.[20]

On the other hand, the notary was obliged even apart from receiving any compensation to draw up for poor clients such legal instruments as were relevant.[21] But even more significant is the fact that the notary was to perform those duties which concerned the procedure of the court, and not such as related to the personal needs of the parties. The *consilia coauditorum,* i.e., the various points of advice which according to the practice the other members of the Rota offered to the auditor who was sitting in the case, were to be taken by the notary.[22] This work was not mentioned in the tax-list of the fees made payable for the performance of various duties on the part of the court notary.[23] From this second point of view, then, the notary was designated for the performance of certain tasks which could be assigned to him for the reason that he was an official designated by the court and functioning under court control.

---

[18] Ioannes XXII, const. *Ratio iuris,* 16 nov. 1331, n. 11—Tangl, p. 86.

[19] Ioannes XXII, const. *Ratio iuris,* 16 nov. 1331, n. 21—Tangl, p. 87.

[20] Tangl, *Iuramentum XI*, p. 46.

[21] Ioannes XXII, const. *Ratio iuris,* 16 nov. 1331, n. 13—Tangl, const. XI, p. 86.

[22] Ioannes XXII, const. *Ratio iuris,* 16 nov. 1331, n. 16—Tangl, p. 86.

[23] Ioannes XXII, const. *Ratio iuris,* 16 nov. 1331, n. 30—Tangl, pp. 88-90.

The bulk of the evidence in the Constitution suggests that it was the vice-chancellor—at that period—who had control of the creation of the judicial notary. If he did not actually make the appointment, he had clearly three important rights in this regard. First of all, it was his duty to examine candidates "*de litteratura et scriptura sufficienti,*" through which they became qualified to exercise the office. Secondly, he was required to satisfy himself "*de vita et conversatione*" of the candidates. In the third place, it was he who received the oath from the notary on his appointment.[24]

In any case, the position of the judicial notary was two-sided, ambiguous. This fact resulted from a haphazard development. From one point of view the notary was independent of the curial organization, designated by and responsible solely to his immediate superior. From the other, he stood directly under the control of the administration. In the case of those notaries who functioned not in the courts of law but in the executive departments of the curia this ambiguity did not obtain.[25]

As things developed, the conflict of rivalries tended to dissolve the ambiguous position of the court notaries, and as the influence of the vice-chancellor over the notarial system began to grow there developed also a greater degree of unity.[26]

Finally, the Pope himself took an interest in and through a special means exerted an influence over the notary in the court. The Bull *Sicut prudens* of Sixtus IX (1471-1484) organized the notaries of the Rota into a college: of the four notaries apportioned to each auditor, one was designated by the Pope, and one each by the vice-chancellor, by the *camerarius*, and by the auditor.[27] Their official character was ultimately recognized.

With the development of the notarial system, formularies were compiled as aids for the notary in his work. The papal formulary

[24] Ioannes XXII, const. *Ratio iuris*, 16 nov. 1331, n. 19—Tangl, const. XI, p. 87.

[25] Ioannes XXII, const. *Qui exacti temporis*, 16 nov. 1331, n. 5—Tangl, const. XIII, p. 112.

[26] Barraclough, *Public Notaries and the Papal Curia* (London: Macmillan & Co., Ltd., 1934), pp. 18, 19. This work is a valuable aid in ascertaining the role of the notary in the papal curia.

[27] Barraclough, *Public Notaries and the Papal Curia*, p. 19, note 3.

as a collection of papal letters, the *rescripta apostolica* and *instrumenta*, was composed for the most part of excerpts from the various *registra*.

The *Formularium Notariorum Curiae Romanae*, composed in 1327, serves as a fine example to illustrate the type of formulary then extant. There were, of course, formularies for notaries outside the curia which preceded this collection. This particular formulary was not only an official compilation, but it was also the first official compilation of its kind. Of the multitudinous notarial formularies which had been produced in the thirteenth century none had filled the double position of a formulary for the notariate and of a formulary for the Curia. Barraclough has made a study of this formulary. Its importance as a model of the formularies cannot be overestimated. Barraclough is of the opinion that "although it is maintained that the '*Formularium Notariorum Curie*' of 1327 preserved its influence for something like a century, it is therefore in no way implied that the development of form and structure in handbooks of this class altogether ceased. . . . On the contrary, the notarial formularies which emanate from the fourteenth-century curia all originate in the work here under disccussion: the ultimate source of all is the collection which we have entitled '*Formularium Notariorum Curie.*' "[28]

The judicial notary seemed to be required to take an added oath, as has been noted above in regard to the *audientia sacri palatii.* The Council of Salzburg in 1386 stressed the oath of office that was required of every notary. The reason advanced by the council was the prevention of the dangers inherent in the hiring of unknown and unskilled notaries.[29]

Baart (1858-1908) reported that there seemed to be no general positive laws requiring the oath of office, but that the universal, immemorable custom, as well as the unanimous teaching of canonists, required the notary to take the oath. Baart held that the omission

[28] *Public Notaries and the Papal Curia*, pp. 91, 92.

[29] Mansi, XXVI, 732: "Placuit nostro sancto concilio, ut nullus se notarium publicum asserens, in officio tabellionatus aliquatenus admittatur, nec credatur eius instrumento nisi coram loci ordinario vel eius officiali de suo officio faciant [sic] plenam fidem, cum saepe ex notariis incognitis et imperitis grandia pericula soleant provenire."

of the oath would undoubtedly render all acts of a notary suspected, if not *ipso facto* null and void, and that the acts of a notary who had not taken the oath of office should be held and had been held null and void.[30]

Notaries set up by apostolic authority multiplied little by little. There was no doubt a tendency, as the system developed, to exclude from the papal curia—and particularly from the courts—all notaries not created by the pope or on his authority. Only papal and imperial notaries could exercise their profession universally. The papal powers —in the thirteenth and fourteenth, if not the fifteenth, century—were used, as it seems, with care and with the genuine intention of providing professional workers of a high class. The right to create notaries *auctoritate apostolica* was rarely granted for more than a stated case.[31] Pope John XXI (1275-1276), for example, empowered the bishop of Albi to create two notaries with apostolic authority, that is, with the title of apostolic notary.[32]

Pope Clement V (1305-1314), the first of the seven Avignon popes of the so-called "Babylonian Captivity," at the petition of the twenty French bishops who had assembled at Vienne for the XV Ecumenical Council (1311-1312), extended to these bishops thc faculty of authorizing two persons as *tabelliones* if they had been found worthy by an examination and had taken an oath of office.[33]

While none but the supreme power in Church and State could by inherent right create notaries, it was the teaching of canonists that by custom, introduced with the consent of the pope, bishops could create notaries for their dioceses. Inasmuch as the bishop only from general custom had this power to create notaries, it follows that he had to perform this act himself and could not delegate it to his

[30] *Legal Formulary* (3. ed., New York: Pustet, 1899), p. 63.

[31] Barraclough, *Public Notaries and the Papal Curia*, p. 13, note 2.

[32] Potthast, *Regesta Pontificum inde ab anno post Christum MCXVIII ad MCCIV* (2 vols., Berolini, 1874-1875), n. 21174 (hereafter cited Potthast).

[33] Mansi, XXV, 398-399. Both the grant and the oath of office are contained here.

[34] Bouix, *Tractatus de Judiciis Ecclesiasticis* (2 vols., Parisiis, 1855), I, 497 (hereafter cited *De Judiciis*); Pirhing, *Ius Canonicum in V Libros Decretalium* (5 vols., Dilingae, 1674-1678), lib. II, tit. 22, n. 8; Baart, *Legal Formulary*, pp. 58-59.

vicar general or to others.[84] A bishop living outside his diocese could not create there a notary or chancellor for his diocese, since the creation of a notary was held to be an act of contentious and not of voluntary jurisdiction.[85]

Article IV. Cleric or Lay?

The matter of salaries afforded the notary provides the preface to the last point in regard to the legislation enacted before the Council of Trent.

As the judicial notary performed various functions in the court, so his salary was determined by the amount of work he performed. The "*Ordo Iudiciarus*" of Aegidius de Fuscaraiis (d. 1289) indicated that it was left to the judge to decide this matter, for it was he who "*debet videre quantum petat notarius pro termino, quantum pro contestatione litis, quantum pro exceptionibus ponendis in actis, quantum pro exemplatione instrumentorum, quantum pro interlocutorio, quantum pro dicto testis, quantum pro sententia. Et sic de omnibus. Et omnia ista el alia quae scribuntur, debet iudex moderare, habito respectu ad magnitudinem vel parvitatem causae et etiam ad facultates litigantium.*"[86]

Pope Boniface VIII (1294-1305) enacted statutes forbidding exorbitant notarial fees and restraining assessors from bleeding notaries of part of their salary.[87] Even the auditors had tried to share in the salary. A correction of this situation was made by Pope Martin V (1417-1431) in the instructions given to his legate at the Council of Basle (1429-30).[88]

More and more the stress on the personal quality and fitness of the notary was brought to the fore. His personal and private life was the subject of legislation as well. Pope John XXII specifically mentioned public concubinage as disqualifying a candidate or an

---

[85] Bouix, *ibid.*, p. 499; Pirhing, *loc. cit.*

[86] Wahrmund, "Der Ordo Iudiciarius des Aegidius de Fuscarariis," *Quellen zur Geschichte des romisch-kanonischen Processes im Mittelalter* (5 vols., Innsbruck and Heidelberg, 1905-1931), III, Part I (1916), p. 122.

[87] C. 11, *de rescriptis*, I, 3, in VI°.

[88] Tangl, Reform I, n. 16, p. 365.

incumbent.[39] Pope Martin V, a hundred years later, in his Constitution *In apostolicae dignitatis* prescribed that the *notarii sacri palatii auditorum* were to dress decently and in garb suitable to a *clericus saecularis,* were to refrain from frequenting the taverns, and were not to live in concubinage, since these matters reflected on their office. The legal sanction that attached to the law was deprivation of the office in the event that the law was violated.[40]

The use of a cleric as judicial notary was the subject of much discussion which stemmed from a decree in which Pope Innocent III prohibited major clerics from acting as notaries in courts of law. The decree was issued in 1211, and was later incorporated in the Decretals of Gregory IX.[41]

The prohibition specifically mentioned major clerics. The object was the *officium tabellionatus.* Failure to observe this legislation was punishable with loss of the benefice the major cleric held. According to Bernard of Parma (d. 1266), the glossator of the Decretals, the prohibition affected clerical judicial notaries in the ecclesiastical as well as in civil courts.[42] The controversy over the interpretation spread over the following centuries.

Could a non-beneficed major cleric be engaged as an ecclesiastical judicial notary? Did the prohibition affect only the secular courts? Were clerics in Minor Orders, beneficed or non-beneficed, similarly affected? To some of the questions an answer was given through the permission by which Pope Clement IV (1265-1268) in 1265 allowed religious and secular clerics, even though in Major Orders, to function as judicial notaries in inquisitorial trials—"*in causis fidei.*"[43]

Hostiensis (d. 1271) listed five reasons why clerics in Major

---

[39] *Ratio iuris,* 16 nov. 1331, n. 22—Tangl, const. XI, p. 87.

[40] 1 sept. 1418, n. 25—Tangl, const. XXVI, p. 141.

[41] C. 8, X, *ne clerici vel monachi saecularibus negotiis se immisceant,* III, 50; Potthast, n. 4337.

[42] *Glossa ordinaria,* ad c. 8, X, *ne clerici vel vel monachi saecularibus negotiis se immisceant,* III, 50, s.v. *clericis in sacris*: "Sed numquam in causa ecclesiatica sive spirituali, coram ecclesiastico iudice, possint esse tabelliones? Videtur quod non, quia simpliciter prohibentur, unde generaliter intelligendum est."

[43] C. 11, *de haereticis,* V, 2, in VI°; Potthast, n. 19379.

Orders were not to function in the capacity of a *tabellio,*[44] but then went on to assert "*quod si non habet beneficium, hoc officio uti potest.*"[45] He taught that the prohibition was not effective *praecise,* but *causative*: that the cleric was either to exercise the office and give up his benefice, or else retain the benefice and cease functioning as *tabellio.*

A lay notary, according to Hostiensis, could not be used in spiritual or ecclesiastical affairs.[46] A secular notary could not be used in ecclesiastical courts, nor could an ecclesiastical notary be employed in secular courts.[47] Moreover, Hostiensis held that a beneficed minor cleric could not be a judicial notary.[48]

The position of Hostiensis was more or less of the same character with that which was later held by Ioannes Andreae (1272-1348), but the latter did not regard the prohibition as affecting minor clerics, even though beneficed. The opinion that a beneficed cleric in Minor Orders who undertook the office of *tabellio* lost both his clerical status and his benefice, like one who married, was rejected by Ioannes Andreae: "*hoc non reciperetur hodie nisi per aliquas circumstantias iustificaretur hoc dictum.*"[49]

Abbas Panormitanus (Nicholaus de Tudeschis, 1386-1453), also known as Abbas Siculus, was opposed to these views. Although in one place in his commentary he stated that a "*clericus constitutus in sacris, non habens beneficium, non prohibetur exercere officium tabellionatus,*" in another place he held that a "*clericus non potest tabellionatus officium exercere, etiam stante consuetudine in contrarium.*"[50]

Later commentators and historians added to the interpretations.

---

[44] *Commentaria in Quinque Decretalium Libros* (5 vols. in 3, Venetiis, 1581), lib. III, tit. 50, *ne clerici vel monachi,* c. 8, s.v: *Sicut te,* n. 1.

[45] *Ibid.,* n. 8.

[46] *Ibid.,* n. 7.

[47] *Summa Aurea* (Venetiis, 1570), lib. III, tit. 50, *ne clerici vel monachi,* c. 8, n. 5.

[48] *Ibid.,* n. 1.

[49] *In Quinque Decretalium Libros Novella Commentaria* (4 vols., Venetiis, 1581), lib. III, tit. 50, c. 6, *Sicut te,* n. 9.

[50] *Commentaria in Quinque Libros Decretalium* (5 vols. in 7, Venetiis, 1588, lib. III, tit. 50, c. 8, n. 8 as opposed to n. 18.

The rigorism of Fagnani (1598-1678) is apparent in his teaching that the prohibition extended to all clerics, in Major and Minor Orders, provided they had a benefice.[51] Basing his arguments chiefly on the concession of Pope Clement IV, Fagnanus made exceptions only *in causis fidei*.[52]

Thomassinus (1619-1695) held that the prohibition related to a secular judge's use of a clerical notary, that it regarded beneficed clerics in Major Orders only, and that the prohibition was restricted to the secular courts of law.[53]

The period immediately prior to the Council of Trent was described by Thomassinus as such that "*iam officium, non ordo notariorum spectetur, cum olim ordo esset, vel minoribus ordinibus aggregarentur, et inter clericos recenserentur notarii, etsi fere nunc laici habeantur. Cum presbyteri, diaconi, aliique spectabiles viri, amplum sibi duxerunt notariorum exercere munera, paulatim illa inolevit opinio, mera ea esse officia, quae indui et exui possent. Cumque clerici coniugati in laicorum tandem, sortem et colluviem fere demersi sint, notarii qui eiusmodi erant clerici, pro laicis et ipsi habiti sunt, et solo nomine clerici.*"[54]

---

[51] *Commentaria in Quinque Libros Decretalium* (5 vols., Venetiis, 1696), lib. III, tit. 50, c. 8, n. 27.

[52] *Ibid.*, n. 28.

[53] *Vetus et Nova Ecclesiae Disciplina circa Beneficia et Beneficiarios*, Pars I, lib. II, c. 106, n. 3.

[54] *Ibid.*, n. 5.

CHAPTER III

FROM THE COUNCIL OF TRENT (1545-1563) TO THE CODE OF CANON LAW (1918)

Article I. Tridentine and Later Conciliar Legislation

The council of Trent (1545-1563) gave to the judicial notary a more stable character, and with this stability came a much higher degree of over-all episcopal control. Incompetency in the notarial system in general seems to have been rampant in the period preceding the Council of Trent. It is easy to understand what harm could result through a judicial notary, or through any notary for that matter, who abused his office, since he was responsible for the accuracy of original records.

In order to obviate the difficulties arising from lack of firm episcopal control over the notarial system, the Council of Trent gave to the bishop the powers necessary to insure the competency of the judicial notary and of notaries in general. An examination by the bishop was one of the means afforded. No notary was exempted from this examination, notwithstanding the fact of his appointment by apostolic, imperial or royal authority. The successful completion of the examination on general fitness for the office was not the only means of controlling the notary, however. If the notary was found to be delinquent in office at any time, the bishop could forbid him to exercise his office in ecclesiastical and spiritual affairs, lawsuits, and causes. The prohibition could be invoked either on a temporary or on a permanent basis. An appeal, if made, remained without the effect of suspending the prohibition of the ordinary. The appointment-designation of the judicial notary and his tenure of office were thus effectively put under the control of the bishop.[1]

[1] Sess. XXII, *de ref.*, c. 10—Schroeder, *Canons and Decrees of the Council of Trent* (St. Louis: B. Herder, 1941), p. 158 (hereafter cited *Council of Trent*).

The Tridentine legislation also included a specific decree concerning the duties of the judicial notary. More and more the legislation of this and the following periods was not only to stress what the notary when employed in ecclesiastical trials was to do, since that was well established and recognized, but was also to place emphasis on and to describe how the notary carried on his functions in an ecclesiastical trial. The Council of Trent decreed that the notary was to furnish the appellant, as soon as possible and within at least one month, a copy of the proceedings of the trial. In the event that through delay the notary became guilty of fraud, he was, at the discretion of the ordinary, to be suspended from the administration of his office and compelled to pay double the costs of the lawsuit. The monetary fine was to be divided between the appellant and the poor of the locality. A suitable fee bound the notary to furnish this copy of the acts to the appellant.[2]

Four councils have been chosen as indicating conciliar legislative thought on this point consequent to the Council of Trent. The I Provincial Council of Milan (1565) enlarged on the Tridentine legislation. The legislation concerning the judicial notary reflects the general excellence of the council as a whole. The council was convened by the saintly cardinal-archbishop of Milan, Charles Borromeo (d. 1584). The council in one section carefully decreed that clerics were not to be *tabelliones* in worldly matters (section XXVI of *pars secunda*). Then, in a later section (XXXII) entitled "*De Notariis et Scribis,*" particular norms were set up for the moderation of the notarial system in the dioceses.

A college of episcopal notaries was established in each diocese of the province of Milan. The number of members constituting the college was to be determined by the needs of the particular diocese. A candidate who was excommunicated, *infamis*, or repelled by law from being a witness, was to be rejected. Moreover, unless he was at least twenty-four years of age and had been a notary for four years, he was not to be admitted to the college. Experience in ordinary notarial work was a prerequisite for the designation as notary in ecclesiastical trials. A tax schedule was to be drawn up within six months of the adjournment of the council. The oath

[2] Sess. XXIV, *de ref.*, c. 20—Schroeder, *Council of Trent*, p. 212.

of office definitely indicated that any notary was eligible for designation to serve as notary in ecclesiastical trials. Pertinent to the judicial notary, the candidate for the notarial college promised in his oath of office the following: 1) that he had not bought his office; 2) that he would be faithful to his work; 3) that he would observe the tax schedule when billing litigants for his services; 4) that he would not act as procurator; 5) that he would not manipulate the schedule of cases to make a certain case fall in his turn; 6) that he would annotate all the acts properly; 7) that no copies would be made without the permission of the bishop; 8) that secrecy would be observed until the case was published and 9) that he would abide by the statutes of the college of notaries.[3]

The Provincial Council of Benevento in 1693 made the actuary or notary (both terms were used) subject to ecclesiastical censures in the event that he mutilated the rendered testimony or failed to transcribe integrally the depositions of the witnesses.[4]

Although the subject was never brought up for action at the Vatican Council (1869-1870), among the *postulata* of the bishops of Naples was the topic of the chancellors and notaries. The qualifications of *cancellarii* and *notarii* were listed as follows: 1) that they be thirty years of age; 2) that at least they have a doctorate *in utroque iure*; 3) that they have made a successful examination on ecclesiastical procedure in civil (the Code calls it "contentious") or criminal trials.[5] The trend seemed to be towards stricter requirements.

The III Plenary Council of Baltimore (1884) ordered ecclesiastical tribunals set up in each diocese in the United States of America.[6] The Council did not list the judicial notary with the ordinary and necessary officials of the tribunal. The chancellor was mentioned among these, however, and he acted as the notary in ecclesiastical

[3] Hardouin, *Acta Conciliorum et Epistolae Decretales ac Constitutiones Summorum Pontificum* (12 vols., Parisiis, 1714-1715), X, 676-678.

[4] Tit. XLIV, cap. II—*Acta et Decreta Sacrorum Conciliorum Recentiorum, Collectio Lacensis* (7 vols., Friburgi Brisgoviae: Sumptibus Herder, 1870-1892), I, 78 d (hereafter cited *Coll. Lac.*).

[5] *Acta et Decreta SS. Conc. Vaticani*, appendix VI—*Coll. Lac.*, VII-I, 800.

[6] Tit. X, cap. I, n. 297—*Acta et Decreta Concilii Plenarii Baltimorensis Tertii, A.D. MDCCCLXXXIV* (Baltimore: John Murphy, 1886), p. 170 (hereafter cited *Acta et Decreta Balt. III*).

trials. In fact, there was a growing custom, fostered by the bishops in the United States, of having their chancellors made civil notaries public. To the chancellor seem to have been assigned most of the notarial duties. In case of necessity a notary or an actuary could be added to the tribunal. It was the chancellor who signed the acts if such a signature was required for validity.[7]

In marriage cases the notary (also referred to as secretary, chancellor, and actuary) was to draw up the entire process. His signature was required on the acts.[8]

The bishop nominated the notary and could suspend or remove him from office.[9] In the criminal cases of clerics the diocesan chancellor was the notary who assisted in the *processus informativus*.[10] The rest of the legislation pertinent to the judicial notary was practically that of the Instruction *Cum magnopere* of 1883, which is to be discussed later.[11]

Article II. Some Features of the Post-Tridentine Legal Thought

A. The Personal Status of the Judicial Notary

The controversy over the question of the employment of lay and clerical notaries which had waxed strong before and during the Tridentine period began to reach a solution in the era following the Council of Trent. With the judicial notary brought under much closer episcopal supervision, the trend in the legal thought began to shift towards clerical notaries and away from lay notaries in ecclesiastical affairs and trials. The question of fees that had helped

---

Tit. X, cap. II, n. 299—*Acta et Decreta Balt. III*, p. 172.

[8] "Notarius (Secretarius, Cancellarius, Actuarius eo praesertim fine constituitur, ut totius processus protocollum excipiat, notando scilicet dicta et facta omnia iudicialia, nominatim interrogationes examinandis factas eorumque responsiones; referendo in actis quidquid ad causam pertinet. Praeterea plura instrumenta in processu conficienda, ut fidem in posterum facere valeant, a notario signata sint oportet, ut appareat ex Instr. S.C. cit."—tit. X, cap. II, n. 305, *Acta et Decreta Balt. III*, p. 175.

[9] Tit. X, cap. II, n. 306—*Acta et Decreta Balt. III*, p. 175.

[10] Tit. X, cap. III, n. 311—*ibid.*, p. 178.

[11] Tit. X, cap. III, nn. 314-315—*ibid.*, pp. 180-181.

to bring the system under fire as it smacked of *negotium* was even matter for legislation by the Council of Trent. Apparently the charge of *negotium* aimed at the system of fees, and which if true made the office unfit for clerics, was losing its force.[12]

Pope Clement VIII (1592-1605) decreed in 1601 that judicial acts sent to Rome when inquisitional cases were involved were to be drawn up gratis by the secretaries, chancellors and notaries.[13]

Ferraris (d. ca. 1763) appealed to custom as the determining factor as to how the notariate was to be regarded in a particular place. For many years, he stated, some authors regarded the office as base and vile (e.g., Fagnani, *supra*). Ferraris, on the other hand, regarded the office as being reputable. The role of custom was exemplified in regard to the situation at Milan, where the notary was and always had been held in high esteem. At Milan the notary could be admitted to the decurionate, to membership in *collegia* and also to other honors. This point as relevant to Milan is especially noteworthy. The notary in Milan seems always to have enjoyed a high reputation. The Milanese rite even placed the notariate among the Minor Orders, a point that has already been made in this study. The careful attention given to the notariate by the I Provincial Council of Milan in 1565 lends added support to the foregoing conclusion. The Milanese were consistent in their attitude. The position of the notary in any given locale was, however, according to Ferraris, to be determined in the light of the extant usage and custom.[14]

Laymen could be employed and were employed as notaries in ecclesiastical trials. Ferraris based this doctrine on the common opinion and the actual practice in many places.[15]

---

[12] Conc. Trident., sess. XXIV, *de ref.*, c. 20—Schroeder, *Council of Trent*, p. 212.

[13] Const. *Sanctissimus Dominus Noster*, 5 ian. 1601—*Magnum Bullarium Romanum* (19 vols., Luxemburgi, 1727-1754), III, n. CXXVI.

[14] *Prompta Bibliotheca Canonica, Iuridica, Moralis, Theologica necnon Ascetica, Polemica, Rubricistica, Historica* (ed. noviss., 9 vols., Romae, 1885-1889), s.v. *Notarius*, nn. 27-32 (hereafter cited *Bibliotheca*).

[15] "Laici possunt esse notarii in negotiis, litibus et causis ecclesiasticis ac spiritualibus. Communis, et patet experientia; pluribus enim in locis actuarii seu cancellarii Episcopi sunt laici"—*Bibliotheca*, s.v. *Notarius seu Cancellarius*, nn. 13-14.

Moral responsibility rested with the notary or the *tabellio.* Lack of sufficient knowledge, violation of the oath of office, the addition or suppression of notable or momentous testimony were regarded as moral matters, as were negligence in keeping the acts when such negligence resulted in damage; delaying a case in order to get more money out of it; the omission of some necessary solemnity such as the date, etc., through malice or neglect; manipulation of the register of cases to be tried, hiding the acts or refusing a party who asked for a copy of the *transumptum processus.*[16]

In his study on notarial responsibility, Laborderie-Boulou noted that Irnerius (1055-1130) developed the first idea of the responsibility of the notary by reason of the things in his charge. Durandus (Durantis, 1237-1296) in his work *Speculum Iuris* added the notion of a notarial responsibility in relation to the question of ignorance regarding the law itself. It was Bartolus (1314-1356) who climaxed the theory: "La responsibilite du notaire pourra, selon Bartole, se trouver engagee dans trois hypothieses principales: pour ignorance du driot, par negligence ou pour incompetence . . . Bartole insiste particulierement sur l'imperitie du notaire et sur les erreurs incorporees aux actes."'[17]

This later development in Roman law is an interesting point to note, since the Imperial Roman law never made notaries civilly responsible for incompetent acts. It did, nevertheless, punish them criminally—sometimes in a cruel manner. An example of this can be found in the Justinian Code legislation which imposed irrevocable exile and loss of all goods.[18]

Reiffenstuel (1642-1703) stressed the importance of competency in the notary. He listed under the headings of efficient, formal, material and final causes the general reasons which furnished grounds for impugning the acts executed by a notary.[19] Applied to the judicial notary, his appointment, his proper functioning, his obser-

[16] Ferraries, *Bibliotheca,* s.v. *Notarius,* n. 26.

[17] "Recherches sur les Origines de la Responsabilite Notariale," *Revue Generale du Droit,* XXXVI (1912), 390.

[18] (1,2) (14,6[3]).

[19] *Ius Canonicum Universum* (7 vols., Parisiis, 1864-1870), lib. II, tit. 22, IX, "De impugnatione instrumentorum, praesertim ob defectum notarii," nn. 256-281.

vance of the solemnities in confecting acts, his title to office, were all involved in the validity of his employment.[20]

Reiffenstuel further enjoined the notary to write only what he had seen and heard.[21]

Although Ferraris in the eighteenth century was able to write that in many places laymen were employed in church courts, one hundred years later Bouix (1808-1870) commented that in his time in many places no laymen were employed in ecclesiastical affairs.[22] The periods from Fagnanus to Ferraris to Bouix represent the current in opinion and practice concerning lay and cleric ecclesiastical employment. Laymen could be notaries or chancellors in spiritual causes. This was commonly admitted.[23]

Bouix defined the notary as the genus, the actuary and the chancellor as a species of the genus, according to particular or general curial duties.[24] Pallottini, writing in the same century, interchanged the terms. It was his opinion that the terms could be used indiscriminately.[25]

Bouix was not convinced that the notariate was ever constituted as a Minor Order in the strict sense.[26] He presented an interesting explanation, however, of the problem of the Decretal prohibition against a cleric's acting as a notary. He viewed the Innocentian prohibition as affecting only the particular locality to which it was addressed. By the time Pope Gregory IX incorporated it in his Decretals, a contrary custom was flourishing and continued to flourish. The legislation on this point never did acquire the force of general law because of this custom. Custom overruled the written law in this matter, and by general and constant practice the use of clerical no-

[20] *Ius Canonicum Universum*, lib. II, tit. 22, n. 27.

[21] *Loc. cit.*

[22] *De Judiciis*, I, 492.

[23] Bouix, *De Judiciis*, I, 501.

[24] *Ibid.*, p. 489.

[25] *Collectio omnium conclusionum et resolutionum quae in causis propositus apud Sacram Congregationem Cardinalium S. Concilii Tridentini Interpretum prodierunt ab eius institutione anno MDLXIV ad annum MDCCCLX, distinctis titulis alphabetico ordine per materias digesta* (17 vols., Romae, 1868-1893), XIV, s.v. *Notarius seu Cancellarius* (hereafter cited *Collectio*).

[26] *De Judiciis*, I, 489.

taries had passed into common law, so that it was licit for any cleric, even one constituted in Major Orders, to be a notary in the ecclesiastical curia. It never became a legitimate position for a cleric in a civil court.[27]

Baart reported that "by the general practice of today [1899], as well as that of former times, it is lawful for clerics, even in major orders, to act as notaries or chancellors for acts of ecclesiastical authority."[28]

B. The Religious Judicial Notary

A papal grant of a privilege to the Dominican Order has been selected to exemplify for purpose of this study the use of a notary in the trials of religious.

Pope Pius V (1566-1572) granted to the Superiors of the Dominican Order and to all others who participated with them in the same privilege the power to create members ("*fratres*") as public notaries, for use in and out of the trials of religious. The appointment could be made for particular as well as general causes. As many as five (in fact, the grant made an arithmetically progressive enumeration) or even more could be selected. The candidate had to be of a high caliber in faith and morals.[29]

In his treatment of religious notaries, Ferraris added the mode and formula for their institution. The candidate knelt in front of two or three witnesses as he gave the oath to his Superior that he would exercise his office faithfully and with all integrity. The Superior then gave him pen and ink, saying these words: "*Accipe potestatem notificandi et intimandi pro ista provincia. . . .*" All was drawn up later in testimonial form.[30]

Ferraris stated it is a common opinion that generals and provincials of religious orders could create notaries for the trials of

---

[27] *Ibid.*, pp. 492-3.

[28] *Legal Formulary*, pp. 60-61.

[29] Const. *Debitum pastoralis*, 21 mart. 1571—*Magnum Bullarium Romanum*, II, n. CXXIV.

[30] *Bibliotheca*, s.v. *Notarius*, nn. 21-22.

religious.[51] Reiffenstuel seemed to indicate that they did not have this power.[52]

C. The Decision of the S.C.C., Ianuen., 31 iul 1819

The case which was presented to the Sacred Congregation of the Council and which was settled through the decision given on July 31, 1819, has been singled out for discussion here for the reason that it contained many points relative to the appointment and designation of the judicial notary.

The issue arose between the archiepiscopal curia of Genoa and a pro-synodal judge who, as an apostolic delegated judge, set aside the chancellor of the Genoa curia and employed a lay notary chosen by himself. The *promotor fiscalis* felt that the archiepiscopal rights had been infringed by this course of action, and the vicar general warned the judge to use the chancellor as notary in this case and in any others. The acts of the case drawn up by the lay notary were to be handed over to the chancellor. The judge, on the other hand, contended that he could use as notary whomever he chose. The case was submitted to the Sacred Congregation of the Council for a solution.

A three-point defense based on custom, canon law, and the brief of delegation was presented. A series of cases was cited. These dated from 1780-1794, in which a lay notary had been used and the diocesan chancellor disregarded. This was adduced in support of the claim that custom favored the judge's action, and that this custom was not reprobated. Canon law also was brought in as support, the claim being based on the decretal legislation which accredited a delegated judge with full power in those things over which he presided.[53] Furthermore, note was taken of the teaching of Ferraris that the *conservatores regularium,* if they were apostolic delegates, were not obliged to use an episcopal notary, but could employ anyone they saw fit. Thus the Sacred Congregation of the Council, in *Faventina iurisdictionis,* 17 dec. 1667, had ruled that the *conservator* could pick a notary *ad sui libitum.* Finally, the defense maintained

---

[51] *Loc. cit.*

[52] *Ius Canonicum Universum,* lib. II, tit. 22, n. 260.

[53] "Quia ex eo quod causa sibi committitur, super (his) omnibus, quae ad causam ipsam spectare noscuntur, plenariam recipit potestatem."—c. 5, X, *de officio et potestate iudicis delegati,* I, 29.

that the brief of delegation implicitly granted the power of choosing a lay notary.

The *promotor fiscalis* answered these charges point for point. In regard to the contrary custom, there was a Resolution of the Council, *in Alben.*, 15 ian. 1656, that a synodal judge in appeal cases was to use the notaries of the episcopal curia. A fourteen-year custom (1780-1794) was not of sufficient duration to prejudice the law. Pope Benedict XIV, in his *De Synodo Dioesesana,* quoted a decree of the Sacred Congregation of the Council of March, 1601, and the Albi ruling in support of the position that delegated judges had no jurisdiction in this matter. In addition to this the Republic of Genoa when in existence had a statute under the rubric "*De Notariis Actuariis*" to the effect that a defendant could demand the removal of a suspect actuary and call in another. By royal law, public notaries could not draw up the *acta iudiciorum,* since this was to be done by secretaries. Hence any other procedure was invalid. Since in Genoa, then, the notary had no official authority to write judicial acts, it was necessary that the archiepiscopal chancellor be employed. It seems that in Genoa at least civil ordinances affected ecclesiastical practice to some degree. The claim that custom supported the action of the judge was refuted as being *contra ius,* as the Sacred Congregation of the Council had defined that synodal judges in delegated cases could not use lay notaries, but had to use the notaries of the episcopal curia.

In regard to the Decretal law, the canon cited by the defense was not understood to mean that delegated judges were empowered to create *notarii or actuarii.* The bishop had complete control of court notaries. The Council of Trent (sess. XXII, *de ref.*, c, 10) confirmed this. The judicial notary had to be approved by the bishop.

The *Faventina* case of 1667 involved *conservatores* and the episcopal forum, and hence episcopal notaries were regarded as suspect and could not be employed. Antedating both of these decisions was the one sent to Pistoia in 1627, which held that judges had a free hand in the matter of notaries.

The solution of the case devolved on whether the Pistoia decree of 1627 or the Albi decision of 1656 was to have precedence, and/or whether the *Faventina* decision of 1667 could be extended to synodal judges. Did the decretal legislation on delegated judges grant the faculty of choosing any notary to function in ecclesiastical trials?

The *dubium* was formulated thus: "An Iudici Pro-Synodali Ioanni Baptistae Bernardo Gandolpho tamquam delegato Apostolico in causa sibi commissa ius competat eligendi et adhibendi notarium laicum, posthabito cancellario curiae Archiepiscopalis in casu, etc. . . . " The answer was "Negative."[84] The Albi decision was upheld. Episcopal control was affirmed.

The power of the delegated judge must be clarified here. The decision *in Pistorien.*, 21 nov. 1627, ruled that a bishop could not order synodal judges in delegated cases to employ only notaries of the episcopal curia. The contradiction between this decision and the one rendered in 1819 is more apparent than real. The decision rendered in 1819 implied the proscription of a lay notary.[85]

D. The S.R.Rota and the Signatura Apostolica

The newly re-established Roman Rota was organized through the legislation *Lex Propria* of June 29, 1908. Specific regulations concerning the judicial notary were given. Provision was made for the appointing of as many notaries as necessary to the *munus* of actuary or chancellor in the work done by this tribunal.[86]

At least two of the actuaries or judicial notaries were to be priests. In the criminal trials of clerics or of religious, priests alone could be employed. The judicial notary was to be chosen from the Rotal College. The election had to be confirmed by the Supreme Pontiff himself.[87]

The judicial notary was to be present at the oath of office of the auditors and their helpers. He was held to the *secretum officii.* Only with the permission of the presiding official or in consequence

---

[84] *Thesaurus Resolutionum Sacrae Congregationis Concilii* (167 vols., Romae, 1718-1908), LXXIX (1819), 231-238.

[85] Pallottini, *Collectio*, XIV, s.v. *Notarius seu Cancellarius*, n. 37, note 1.

[86] Lex propria S.R.Rota et Signatura Ap., 29 iun. 1908 (*Lex propria*), can. 5, § 1—*Acta Sanctae Sedis* (41 vols., Romae, 1865-1908), XLI (1908), 442 (hereafter cited *ASS*).

[87] *Lex propria,* can. 5, §§ 2-3—*ASS*, XLI (1908), 442.

of the mandate of the dean was he allowed to extract documents from the archives.[38]

One of the notaries of the tribunal was to be present at the *disputatio*. The notary was allowed to inform the parties of the dispositive part of the sentence. He signed the case. At least one priest-notary was assigned to aid the secretary in drawing up the acts, and to serve for the custody of the archives.[39]

The rules to be observed in the Rota were issued two years later.[40] At the examination of the witnesses one notary was always required to be present. He took down the testimony in writing, and after this he proceeded to read back the responses and then signed the acts.[41]

In the trial itself his presence was always required so that he could take down all the acts. At the end, before the signing, he read the acts back to the parties who were then allowed to add or correct anything that needed to be added or corrected. This was the procedure with witnesses.[42]

The Signatura did not require the selection of a notary from the notarial college. One was chosen from the body of the officials and deputed as notary to take down the proceedings in writing and to sign the acts. His signature certified the acts as authentic.[43]

ARTICLE III. SPECIFIC TYPES OF TRIALS

The final point for examination in this historical synopsis of the judicial notary in the pre-Code law will be centered around his activity in two specific types of trials: the criminal trials of clerics, and matrimonial causes. The emphasis will be on the legislation of

---

[38] *Lex propria*, cans. 7, 3, 10—*ASS*, XLI (1908), 442-443.

[39] *Lex propria*, cans. 30, 32, 36—*ASS*, XLI (1908), 450-454.

[40] *Regulae servandae in iudiciis apud S.R.Rotae Tribunal*, 4 aug. 1910—*Acta Apostolicae Sedis, Commentarium Officiale* (Romae, 1909——), II (1910), 7783-850 (hereafter cited *AAS*).

[41] *Regulae servandae in iudiciis apud S.R.Rotae Tribunal*, 4 aug. 1910, § 114, n. 7—*AAS*, II (1910), 821.

[42] *Regulae servandae in iudiciis apud S.R.Rotae Tribunal*, 4 aug. 1910, § 144—*AAS*, II (1910), 827.

[43] *Regulae servandae in iudiciis apud Supremae Signaturae Ap. Tribunal*, 6 mart. 1912, art. 14, 25, 36—*AAS*, IV (1912), 191-198.

the latter part of the nineteenth century, as the crystallization and summation of the position and function of the notary in trials immediately preceding the promulgation of the present Code law. General features emerge to delineate the final phase of the historical development of the office of the judicial notary.

A. The Criminal Trials of Clerics

Prior to the Instruction of the Sacred Congregation of Bishops and Regulars in 1880, by which the Holy See allowed bishops in European countries to conduct summary trials in criminal causes of ecclesiastics on condition that it was impossible or inexpedient to carry out the ordinary trial, a number of decrees mentioned the notary to be employed. The following is a synthesis of the legislation.

A lay chancellor could only materially make out the acts of the proceedings, without exercising directly or indirectly any act of jurisdiction.[44] A lay chancellor for such causes was employed by way of exception.[45] If a layman was used he was not to sign the interrogation and the depositions of the witnesses.[46] It was necessary that a judge-auditor examine the witness. If a notary attempted to examine any witness alone, without a judge-auditor, the proceedings were null.[47] The accused could object to a chancellor on the grounds of suspicion of hostility. In such an event the ordinary was to name another notary for the court.[48]

The original acts of a case were to be kept in the chancery. A copy was given to the accused and was to be certified by the notary or the chancellor.[49] The poor were afforded copies of the acts free of charge. A page consisted of eighteen lines, with twelve syllables to a line.

---

[44] S. C. Ep. et Reg., 30 iun. 1832—*Analecta Iuris Pontificii* (Roame, 1855-1869; Parisiis, 1872-1891), XIII (1874), 46 (hereafter cited *AIP*).

[45] Droste-Messmer, *Canonical Procedure in Disciplinary and Criminal Cases of Clerics* (New York: Benziger, 1887), p. 59, note 4.

[46] S. C. Ep. et Reg., 24 iul. 1832—*AIP*, XIII (1874), 46. This and the immediately preceding instruction *supra* were meant for a particular case in which, according to the bishop-petitioner, the requisite competent clerics were lacking.

[47] S. C. Ep. et Reg., 25 sept. 1806—*AIP*, XIII (1874), 46.

[48] S. C. Ep. et Reg., 2 aug. 1804—*AIP*, XIII (1874), 46.

[49] S. C. Ep. et Reg., 27 iul. 1759—*AIP*, III (1874), 51.

In France the fee for each page was in 1721 set at 2½ *sous*[60] This make-up of a page was confirmed in 1807.[61]

The Instruction of 1880 required that the compiling of the process be entrusted to a capable and competent ecclesiastic ("*probo atque idoneo ecclesiastico*") as actuary.[62] In sections thirty-four and thirty-five the chancellor was spoken of as being present at the process. The question then arose as to who was the actuary referred to in section twelve. The official commentary on the Instruction held that by actuary was understood the chancellor. The teachings of Bouix (*De Iudiciis,* I, pars. II, sec. 2, cap. 15, n. 3) and of Cardinal De Luca (*De Iudiciis,* disc. 5, n. 1) were given as the basis for this view.[63]

Droste-Messmer held that the term actuary did not necessarily imply the chancellor, since section twelve of the Instruction treated of a situation different from the one treated in section thirty-four. When the III Plenary Council of Baltimore (tit. X, cap. II, n. 311) adopted a contrary opinion, Droste-Messmer considered it to be a directive norm at most.[64]

The auditor was free to choose his actuary if the judge, bishop or vicar general allowed this selection.[65]

This canonical summary procedure was allowed to the United States of America in 1883 absolutely and unconditionally.[66] The regu-

---

[60] S. C. Ep. et Reg., mense aug. 1721—*AIP*, XIII (1874), 51.

[61] S. C. Ep. et Reg., 1 oct. 1807—*AIP*, XIII (1874), 46.

[62] S. C. Ep. et Reg., instr. 11 iun. 1880, n. 12—*Codicis Iuris Canonici Fontes*, cura Emi Petri Card. Gasparri editi (9 vols., Romae [postea Civitate Vaticana]: Typis Polyglottis Vaticanis, 1923-1939; Vols. VII-IX ed. cura et studio Emi Iustiniani Card. Seredi), n. 2005 (hereafter cited *Fontes*).

[63] "Ergo cum ad processus confectionem *Actuarii* assessio necessaria edicitur, intelligendum est curiae Cancellarii praesentiam requiri: nam Cancellarii nomen communiter pro Actuario usurpatur, et vicissim."—*ASS*, XV (1882), 386.

[64] *Canonical Procedure in Disciplinary and Criminal Cases of Clerics*, p. 59, note 1.

[65] Droste-Messmer, *loc. cit.* Cf. Rota, *Enchiridion Confessarii et Iudicis Ecclesiastici* (Taurini-Marietti, 1884), n. 64: "Non est ergo necesse, quod assumatur, vel creetur Notarius, sed sufficit Actuarius, seu grapharius, praesidente iudice vel alio delegato ab ipso."

[66] *Fontes*, n. 4900; *Collectanea S. Congregationis de Propaganda Fide* (2 vols., Romae: Typographia Polyglotta, S. C. de Propaganda Fide, 1907), n. 1586

lations of the Instruction of 1883 relative to the judicial notary were essentially the same as those given to the European countries in 1880.[57]

An Instruction of the Holy Office in 1890 put an end to the controversy regarding the use of lay notaries or chancellors in the trials of clerics. Always the chancellor or notary was to be a cleric.[58]

Only fit and competent clerics could be notaries. They needed a good reputation and above all had to be free of the suspicion of corruptibility. The appointment was made by a bishop or prelate *nullius,* and was limited territorially; it extended only to those acts for which the notary was deputed. Appointments made by religious superiors held only for the causes tried in the religious institute.[59]

B. *Matrimonial Causes*

The position of the judicial notary (he was often called chancellor in the Instructions) in marriage causes was basically contained in an Instruction of the Holy See in 1840.[60] Questions were to be proposed in a progressive order. The *interrogata ex officio* introduced by the judge or the *defensor vinculi* (*defensor validitatis matrimonii*) interrupted this order; these questions were to be inserted before the regular order of questions was resumed. The entire deposition was to be read aloud at the end, clearly and intelligibly, and the party was allowed to make any called for alterations before signing. The party, the judge, the *defensor* and chancellor signed the testimony. The chancellor was to be present at the physical examination proceedings in a cause "*super rato et non consummato.*" The

(hereafter cited *Collectanea*) ; Smith, *The New Procedure in Criminal and Disciplinary Causes of Ecclesiastics in the United States* (2. ed., New York: Pustet, 1888) ; Droste-Messmer, *op. cit.*, especially for a comparison of the two Instructions.

[57] S. C. Ep. et Reg., instr. 11 iun. 1880, nn. 12, 34, 35: S. C. de Prop. Fide, instr. a. 1883, nn. XII, XXXIV, XXXV.

[58] S. C. S. Off., instr. 20 iul. 1890: "Cancellarii seu notarii (qui semper ecclesiastici esse debent) . . ." *Fontes*, n. 1123.

[59] Heiner, *De Processu Criminali Ecclesiastico* (edidit A. Wynen, Romae: Pustet, 1912), pp. 19-20.

[60] S. C. C., instr. 22 aug. 1840—*Fontes*, n. 4069.

Instruction gave detailed information and directives on this particular type of process.

The chancellor of the episcopal curia, who acted as the actuary, faithfully recorded the testimony of the experts.[61]

In the ordinary matrimonial trial, the chancellor again acted as judicial notary. His functions were of the same nature as those described in reference to criminal trials. He signed the testimony along with the witness, judge and *defensor*. He also signed the decree of publication of the sentence.[62]

---

[61] S. C. S. Off., instr. a. 1858—*Collectanea*, n. 1153.

[62] S. C. de Prop. Fide, instr. a. 1883, nn. 4, 6, 13, 14, 15, 22.—*Fontes*, n. 4901; *Collectanea*, n. 1587; S. C. S. Off., instr. (ad Ep. Rituum Orient.) a. 1883—*Fontes*, n. 1076.

CHAPTER IV

THE OFFICE OF THE JUDICIAL NOTARY UNDER THE CODE

ARTICLE 1. THE PRESCRIPTION OF CANON 1585

Canon 1585, ‡1. Cuilibet processui interesse oportet notarium qui actuarii officio fungatur; adeo ut nulla habeantur acta, si actuarii manu non fuerint exarata, vel saltem ab eo subscripta.

‡2. Quare iudex, antequam causam cognoscere incipiat, in actuarium assumere debet unum e notariis legitime constitutis, nisi ipse Ordinarius aliquem pro ea causa iam designaverit.[1]

The important role that the judicial notary occupies in ecclesiastical judicial procedure under the Code of Canon Law represents the continuing development of his office.

At every process, and under the sanction of explicit invalidity of the acts for the failure to observe this prescription, there must be present a notary who acts in the capacity of actuary, or recorder, and who at least signs each act. Since no distinction is made about the type of process, even administrative processes are included.[2] This recording notary, or *notarius actuarius*, is the notary who is called herein the judicial notary.[3]

The law admits of no exception: "*cuilibet processui.*" There is no option as to the presence of a judicial notary in ecclesiastical trials.

---

[1] *Codex Iuris Canonici Pii X Pontificis Maximi iussu digestus Benedicti Papae XV auctoritate promulgatus* (Romae: Typis Polyglottis Vaticani, 1917).

[2] Udalricus Beste, *Introductio in Codicem* (ed. altera, Collegeville, Minn.: St. John's Abbey Press, 1944), p. 769.

[3] The explanation for the assumption of this terminology—the judicial notary—is found in the preface to this study. It is submitted respectfully that this standardization of expression which clearly and adequately defines the notary employed in ecclesiastical judicial processes will in time eliminate the confusing use of terms.

All acts are forthwith considered invalid unless they have been drawn up by the judicial notary or, at least, signed by him.

Since this is so, before the beginning of a cause the judge must designate one of the lawfully appointed notaries for the cause, unless the ordinary himself has already selected one for the particular case. The necessity of the employment of a judicial notary is thus clearly established.

Before proceeding to the study of the office of the judicial notary and his functions, one will look to the *finis legis* as affording a guiding principle for the commentary on the law itself. In an allocution delivered on October 2, 1944, to the auditors, officials and ministers of the Sacred Roman Rota and to its advocates and procurators, His Holiness Pope Pius XII declared that "all those who have part in the trial, without exception, must make their action converge to the one end: *pro rei veritate!*"[4] Procedural norms have been established in order to secure a correct manner of administering justice. There must be certainty, therefore, that these norms have been diligently and legitimately observed. It is only fitting that in order to secure these ends there be designated a person, independent of the parties and judge, who will accurately record whatever is said or done in the course of the process to discover the truth and to administer justice. The judicial notary will attest to the veracity of all that transpires. Since he is by law a qualified witness who testifies to the authenticity of the acts of the process, his certification of such acts accords public faith to these. Thus the acts form a permanent authentic record of a process. "*Pro rei veritate*" properly applies to the judicial notary, and perhaps to him even more so than to any other official of the diocesan tribunal.

Article 2. The Appointment and Designation of the Judicial Notary

Before a judge begins the construction of a process, he must select or designate a judicial notary from the body of lawfully ap-

[4] "Matrimonial Trials in Relation to the Ends of the Church," *AAS*, XXXVI (1944), 281; T. Lincoln Bouscaren, *The Canon Law Digest, Supplement through 1948* (Milwaukee: Bruce, 1949), p. 235.

pointed judicial notaries. An exception to this freedom of selection or designation obtains when the ordinary himself designates a particular judicial notary for a particular case.

Since the judicial notary is by nature a notary first of all, and then designated for a process, it is necessary to ascertain the structure of the notarial system from which he springs and is a part, and the provisions contained in the legislation which have special bearing for such a notary who is specifically determined as the judicial notary.

A. Appointment

Canon 1585, ‡2, empowers a judge to choose a notary from the ones lawfully constituted. The canon does not provide for appointment by a judge, but only for the designation of one already declared or constituted as eligible for the position. It is necessary to distinguish here the terms employed. The legislation and commentators seem to have no fixed terminology. For the purposes of this study, "appointment" will refer to the actual constitution in office, while "designation" will signify the selecting, the assuming or the choosing of the already appointed judicial notary. The first problem presented by canon 1585 revolves around the problem of appointing a judicial notary.

Who can appoint an eligible notary? The term "eligible" is not out of place in this regard. For according to the provision of canon 373, ‡2, a notary can be appointed for all and any acts, or for judicial acts only, or for the acts of only a certain *causa* or administrative matter. The appointment of a notary can be such as to exclude his functioning in ecclesiastical trials. To be eligible for designation as the judicial notary in a process, the letter or manner of appointment of a notary must specify or at least not exclude the fact of his appointment or general eligibility for processual cases of a judicial character.

The following have ordinary power to appoint a judicial notary:

a) The pope holds this power[5] for the universal Church, although he is not accustomed to exercise it;[6]

[5]Canon 218.

[6]Roberti, *De Processibus*, I, n. 118.

b) the bishop clearly has this power. The Code of Canon Law employs the term "*Episcopus*" and not "*Ordinarius*", it must be noted;[7]

c) the apostolic administrator permanently constituted has the same rights as a residential bishop;[8]

d) abbots and prelates *nullius,* in being included under the term "bishop"[9] have the same powers as the residential bishop has;[10]

e) In clerical exempt religious institutes the major superiors[11] can appoint notaries, but only for cases relating to the religious communities in which they are superiors.[12]

It does not seem that the vicar general can proceed to the appointment of a notary by ordinary power. Doheny says that perhaps even the vicar general can appoint a judicial notary.[13] Coronata restricts for the vicar general his power of removing the notary from his office to that case in which the vicar general has himself appointed the notary,[14] and seems furthermore to support the view of Santamaria that by law such a power of appointment is not granted to the vicar general.[15] This negative opinion was also supported by August Couly, who held that, if an appointment was made by the vicar general without a special mandate from the bishop, the action was absolutely null.[16]

Coronata and Santamaria[17] and Couly[18] affirm that the vicar capitular cannot, in virtue of his ordinary powers alone, proceed to

---

[7] Canon 373, § 1.

[8] Canon 315, § 1.

[9] Canon 215, § 2.

[10] Canon 323, § 1.

[11] Canon 488, n. 8.

[12] Canon 503.

[13] *Practical Manual for Marriage Cases* (Milwaukee: Bruce Publishing Co., 1938), p. 127.

[14] *Institutiones Iuris Canonici* (5 vols., ed. altera aucta et emendata, Taurini: Marietti, 1939-1947), I, n. 426, footnote 7 (hereafter cited *Institutiones*).

[15] *Ibid.*, n. 427, footnote 4.

[16] "L'Officialite: Les Notaires ou Actuaires," *Le Canoniste Contemporain*, (Paris, 1876-1922); *Le Canoniste* (Paris, 1924-1926), XLVII (February, 1925), 83.

[17] *Institutiones*, I, n. 427, footnote 9. Coronata quotes Santamaria.

[18] *Art. cit., loc. cit.*

such an appointment. Lega-Bartoccetti, however, are of the opinion that, if with a process already instituted an actuary (judicial notary) is lacking and the seat is vacant, the judge can in such a case look to the vicar capitular for appointing a judicial notary, so that the *causa* could be continued without delay.[19]

Since the law allows a judge to designate a notary only if the latter is selected from the legitimately appointed notaries, any power a judge may have in regard to the appointment of a judicial notary must have been delegated. Can a judge when delegated as a judge by the Holy See appoint a judicial notary without special delegated powers to do so? It could seem that the provision "*eligere et assumere*" of canon 1607, ‡1, gives such a judge the faculty to appoint and designate a person who is not already a notary. But *eligere* and *assumere* mean *per se* to select and choose one from several already appointed notaries. The text supports the view that the delegated apostolic judge cannot appoint a notary, but that he can merely designate a judicial notary for the process which he is conducting. In practice, unless the rescript states otherwise and gives such power, it seems that the prescript of the law should be understood, at least in regard to the judicial notary, to allow such a delegated judge no further authority than that of designating a notary.[20] Roberti, on the contrary, holds the affirmative view, namely that a judge delegated by the Holy See can appoint a notary.[21]

The *Officialis,* although he possesses ordinary judicial power, yet he is not an *Ordinarius* in the sense of canon 198, ‡2, and hence he can appoint a judicial notary only when such power has been duly delegated to him by the bishop.

The appointment of the judicial notary should be put down in writing.[22] Failure to observe this formality, however, does not affect the validity of the acts later drawn up by the judicial notary.

---

[19] *Commentarius in Iudicia Ecclesiastica iuxta Codicem Iuris Canonici* (3 vols., Romae: Anonima Libraria Cattolica Italiana, 1938-1941), I, 148 (hereafter cited *Commentarius*).

[20] Lega and Bartoccetti, *Commentarius*, I, 148.

[21] *De Processibus*, I, n. 118.

[22] Canon 364, § 1; canon 159.

B. Designation

As a general rule, it is the judge who makes the designation of a judicial notary for a process by selecting one of the lawfully appointed judicial notaries. The judge as such, in virtue of his office alone, does not have the power to appoint a notary. This faculty must have been delegated to him. The bishop makes the appointments to the list of the judicial notaries, although he may delegate the power to name notaries at least for individual cases.

An exception to this general rule is found in canon 1770, ‡2, n. 4, where the law envisions difficulties in the securing of testimony and explicitly empowers the judge to appoint anyone to function as the judicial notary for the purpose of recording the testimony.[23]

The selection of a notary by the judge is curtailed, of course, when the bishop himself has already designated particular judicial notaries.

A singular exception to the rule of appointment and designation is found in the *Instruction* of the S. C. of the Sacraments, in *De Processibus in Causis Dispensationis super Matrimonio Rato et Non-consummato.*[24] Where such circumstances do not allow for a judicial notary, the delegated one-man commission performs the functions of auditor and notary.

The designation of the judicial notary should precede the actual opening of a process.

Any judge, it appears, can designate a judicial notary, since the Code of Canon Law does not distinguish or discriminate.[25] In the causes of nullity of the marriage bond the *praeses* of the diocesan tribunal is directed to designate the judicial notary.[26]

C. The Oath of Office

Upon appointment, the judicial notary must take an oath to fulfill his office properly and faithfully, apart from all personal discrimination, and to observe secrecy.[27] The Code of Canon Law does not state whether it suffices that the oath of office be taken the first

[23] ". . . ut cum assistentia alicuius, qui actuarii munere fungatur . . ."

[24] Cap. IV, n. 24, § 4.—*AAS*, XV (1923), 397.

[25] Coronata, *Institutiones*, III, n. 1123.

[26] Instruction *Provida* of the S. C. of the Sacraments, 1936, art. 17.

[27] Canon 364, § 2, n. 1.

time a tribunal is constituted, or whether this oath must be taken each time a process is instituted. It should be noted, however, that in a process for a dispensation *super rato et non-consummato* the diocesan tribunal is delegated each time for a particular cause. Hence, the appointments and the oaths of office must be given at the first session of every new cause, even if the same members are delegated for all causes that are handled by a tribunal.[28] Noval (1861-1938) required a renewal of the oath at each separate trial by the judge delegated by the Holy See or by the ordinary judge in an exempt clerical religious institute, according to the provisions of canon 1621, ‡2.[29] Benedetti, however, states that, if a notary has been appointed *ad universitatem causarum*, then it suffices that the oath be taken by him before he enters upon his office; otherwise, it should be taken each time.[30] In any event, "the Bishop can oblige all the members of his tribunal to renew their oaths of office every year. In fact, some dioceses formally open the judicial sessions each year with Solemn Mass and other appropriate church services, after which the oaths are taken. Every year the S. Roman Rota has a similar ceremony at the Vatican, usually during the month of October."[31]

Roberti lists the notary among those who, if they constitute a permanent tribunal, take the oath of office at the time of their appointment. He makes no mention of the repetition of the oath.[32] Doheny holds that one oath suffices for the entire duration of office for members of the tribunal, unless the ecclesiastical authorities or the diocesan statutes determine otherwise.[33]

Despite the fact that the oath of office is demanded by the Code, the validity of a process or of the acts of the cause is not affected by

---

[28] Cf. Decree of the S. C. of the Sacraments, 1923, cap. III, n. 19—*AAS*, XV (1923), 395.

[29] *Commentarium Codicis Iuris Canonici*, Liber IV, *De Processibus*, Pars. I, *De Iudiciis* (Augustae Taurinorum-Romae, 1920), n. 208 (hereafter cited *De Iudiciis*).

[30] *Ordo Iudicialis Processus Canonici super Nullitate Matrimonii Instruendi* (2. ed., Taurini: Marietti, 1938), p. 25.

[31] Doheny, William, *Canonical Procedure in Matrimonial Cases, Vol. I, Formal Judicial Procedure* (second edition, Milwaukee: Bruce Publishing Co., 1948), I, 79 (hereafter cited *Formal Procedure*).

[32] *De Processibus*, I, n. 154.

[33] *Practical Manual for Marriage Cases*, p. 129.

the omission of the oaths. If the oaths are forgotten or omitted, the proceedings and the acts are valid.[34]

It is to be noted also that the judicial notary, besides being obliged to take the oath of office, is bound to make the profession of faith and to take the oath against Modernism.[35] The Code does not mention the latter because of its temporary character, but this oath and the profession of faith accompanying it are still of universal obligation.[36]

The profession of faith which accompanies the oath against Modernism must also be made. The formula for this profession may be found printed at the beginning of the Code. It is not to be confused with the profession of faith in use by reason of the prescription of liturgical laws, e.g., at the reception of converts, baptism.

Canavan is very emphatic about the necessity of these oaths and clearly distinguishes them. "It seems clear from the wording of the *motu proprio* [*Sacrorum Antistitum*] that these [members of the tribunal who have already made the profession of faith by reason of some other dignity or benefice] are required to make a new profession of faith *and* [italics inserted] take the oath against Modernism upon their appointment to the curia or tribunal. This would be consonant with the prescriptions of canon 1406, ‡2, which demands a new profession of faith when one receives a new appointment even of the same kind."[37]

Mathias, in treating of notaries in general, expressly states that the notary is not obliged either to make the profession of faith or to take the oath against Modernism.[38] This is in direct opposition to the view of Canavan, who expressly mentions the notary in the list of those who are required to take both oaths.[39]

---

[34] Doheny, *Formal Procedure*, pp. 79-80.

[35] S. C. S. Off., const. *Pascendi*, 8 sept. 1907, *Fontes*, n. 680; S. C. S. Off., *motu proprio, Sacrorum Antistitum*, 1 sept. 1910, *Fontes*, n. 689, and *AAS*, II (1910), 669.

[36] S. C. S. Off., 22 mart. 1918, *AAS*, X (1918), 136.

[37] *The Profession of Faith*, The Catholic University of America Canon Law Studies, n. 151 (Washington, D. C.: The Catholic University of America Press, 1942), p. 114.

[38] *The Diocesan Curia* (Madras: Good Shepherd Press, 1947), p. 43.

[39] *Op. cit., loc. cit.*

According to canon 1622, § 1, the manner employed in the taking of an oath postulates an invoking of the divine Name, and if the judicial notary is a priest, he places his hand on his breast. A lay judicial notary places his hand on a book of the Gospels.

Article III. The Judicial Notary in Relation to Other Members of the Diocesan Tribunal

A. The Chancellor

Since the chancellor is a notary in virtue of his office,[40] the judge may designate him as the judicial notary for a trial. In the United States, the diocesan chancellor has become a unique personage of administrative ability, distinction, influence and power. His principal duties according to canon law are to keep the acts of the curia in the archives, to arrange them in chronological order, and to make an index of the same.[41] He is not by his appointment to office necessarily designated also as a judicial notary. Like any other notary who has been appointed, he needs a designation.[42] But like any other notary who has been appointed *ad universitatem causarum,* he does not require a new appointment in order to be designated a judicial notary.

B. The Court Secretary

Vaughan reports that in several dioceses of the United States there has gradually come into being a new officer, a notary whose responsibility continues apart from causes and who is known as the secretary of the court.[43]

---

[40] Canon 372, § 3.

[41] Canon 372, § 1.

[42] John Prince, *The Diocesan Chancellor,* The Catholic University of America Canon Law Studies, n. 167 (Washington, D. C.: The Catholic University of America Press, 1942), p. 80.

[43] *Constitutions for Diocesan Courts,* The Catholic University of America Canon Law Studies, n. 210 (Washington, D. C.: The Catholic University of America Press, 1944), p. 39.

The distinction between the judicial notary and the secretary of the court is not found in the Code, but it is in no way contrary to the Code. In order to resolve any confusion that might result in having these two distinct offices in a tribunal, Vaughan suggests that the Constitution of a diocesan court might mention that the actuary (to whom the judicial notary corresponds) performs everything demanded by the Code during the actual trial itself. "He cares for the portfolio of the cause and keeps all records and documents therein. Likewise he notifies all officers of the time and place of the sessions, if necessary, and carefully keeps the minutes of the session even though a stenographer is employed to record the testimony being heard."[44]

The office of the secretary of the court answers a specific need in some dioceses, especially the larger ones. The bishop is free to institute such an office by diocesan law, if he so desires. The secretary should be, of course, made at least a notary.[45] Vaughan suggests that some of the duties to be assigned the secretary of the court might be the following:

"a) To assist the *officialis* in all his judicial and administrative activities;

b) To care for all correspondence of the court;

c) To care for records of appointments by entering these in the register of the roster;

d) To note in the protocol book the day and hour of the reception of causes, commissions and documents as well as the date of fulfillment of causes and commissions;

e) To be present at and record in the register of the roster the oaths of all permanent officers;

f) To care for the seal and to check the presence of the seal and signatures on all documents;

g) To prepare the annual reports for the Holy See and for the bishop;

h) To fulfill other duties given him by the bishop or the *officialis*, such as notifying officers of their appointments to '*turni*'."[46]

---

[44] *Constitutions for Diocesan Courts*, p. 41.

[45] Vaughan, *Constitutions for Diocesan Courts*, p. 40.

[46] *Op. cit.*, pp. 40-41.

The distinction between the judicial notary and the court secretary must be noted and kept in mind. If the latter type of officer gains in popularity, it would seem to provide another reason for establishing the terminology with a view to identifying the notary who is employed in the actual trial itself for the purpose of writing up, certifying, and caring for the acts of a cause, as *the judicial notary*.

C. *Offices Incompatible With That of the Judicial Notary*

The role of the judicial notary always constitutes a distinct office, even in summary cases. The office of judicial notary is, therefore, incompatible with that of judge, instructor, promoter of justice, *defensor vinculi*, advocate, or procurator.[47] Although the offices of judge and auditor were called everywhere incompatible with that of the judicial notary, no word occurs in the decretalists of the incompatibility of the office of notary and advocate. The two offices are incompatible, however, since the combination of the two could give rise to the exception of suspicion. One and the same person could be a judicial notary and an advocate, but he could not function as both in the same procedure. In practice the holding of both offices by one and the same person should be avoided.[48]

Even though other members of the court might under certain circumstances perform the physical act of committing court records to writing, none could lawfully supplant or substitute the judicial notary. In such cases of assistance, the acts would have the value of the lawful judicial acts if the judicial notary was present and signed the acts, since his subscription would fulfill the requirements of the law.

The exceptional case of a one-man delegated commission gathering testimony in sparsely populated or unsettled districts for cases of ratified, non-consummated marriages has been noted above. It would seem hard to justify, however, the practice in some instances wherein a priest when delegated to gather some testimony requested

---

[47] Roberti, *De Processibus*, I, n. 117; Coronata, *Institutiones*, III, n. 1123; S. C. Ep. et Reg., apr. 1727—*AIP*, XIII (1874), 44.

[48] A. Toso, "*An Notarii et Advocati Munera Incompatibilia Sint in Causis Ecclesiasticis?*", *Jus Pontificium* (Romae; 1921-1940), XVIII (1938), 81-84.

by the court proceeds to do so without anyone to witness what transpires, even though he be not appointed as a duly authorized notary. It seems desirable for the court to include proper instructions when sending out a questionnaire. Processual norms are reasonable rules. Such evidence and testimony as is needed should be obtained in the required manner. Where not all the points of law can be observed because of peculiar circumstances, the resulting deviations should be noted in the acts, but they should not stand in the way of the gathering of testimony that may be very valuable for the cause at issue.

Article IV. The Competency of the Judicial Notary

The function of the notary is that of a qualified witness. It is of the office of the notary when he is employed in ecclesiastical trials to testify to the authenticity of the acts of the cause being heard.[49] This office does not carry with it any power of jurisdiction.[50] Since he lacks judicial power, the judicial notary should abstain from the exercise of power proper to the judge alone. The acts drawn up by the notary in legal form merit public faith. The law sets up a presumption regarding the public faith to be accorded such acts.[51] Competency is spoken of here not in the sense of the limited extent of the needed jurisdiction, but in the sense of the limits within which the presumption of public faith obtains upon the fulfillment of the prerequisite conditions. The notary can write or compose only such documents for which he has been authorized.[52] A judicial act or document composed by a notary who had been appointed for administrative affairs only would be invalid.[53]

---

[49] While the notariate is not an ecclesiastical office in the strict sense, it does fulfill the conditions required by canon 145 to qualify as an office in the wide sense. Cf. Coronata, *Institutiones*, I, n. 427, 3°.

[50] Roberti, *De Processibus*, I, n. 117; Coronata, *Institutiones*, III, n. 1123.

[51] F. X. Wernz, and P. Vidal, *Ius Canonicum* (7 tomes in 8 vols., Vol. VI, *De Processibus*, Romae: Apud Aedes Universitatis Gregorianae, 1927), VI, 107. Cf. Canons 1813, § 1, n. 2; 1814; 1816.

[52] Canon 374, § 2.

[53] Charles Augustine, *A Commentary on the New Code of Canon Law* (8 vols., Vol. II, 3. ed., St. Louis: B. Herder and Co., 1919), II, 410-411.

The competency of a judicial notary is further limited in consequence of a territorial element or factor. He can draw up acts worthy of public faith only in the territory of the superior who lawfully appointed him.[64] A notary who would attempt to perform his duties in a strange territory would lack the proper authorization and would therefore act invalidly.[65] This territorial limitation of competency affects the validity of the acts.[66] In the treatment of this matter it is necessary to keep in mind that the acts of a lawfully appointed notary are valid universally. The point of law at issue here is the place where these acts are drawn up and how this factor affects the confection of judicial acts in regard to validity.

This rule of territorial competency in canon 374, § 2, is based on the nature of episcopal jurisdiction. This episcopal jurisdiction is strictly limited according to the axiom: "*extra territorium ius dicenti non paretur impune.*"[67] An opinion under the earlier law, in which the power of a bishop was not determined in express words, according to Lega and Bartoccetti held that a notary could exercise his office extraterritorially if asked by the subjects of the one who had appointed him.[68] This opinion cannot any longer be sustained. Lega and Bartoccetti seem to indicate that the basis for the present law can not be found in the older law, but is explained on the basis of historical reasons and conclusions sustained by authors of great note.[69]

As an exception to this territorial competency, Roberti holds that, when a notary assists a bishop who either has been expelled from his territory or has been impeded from exercising his jurisdiction in his territory, under such circumstances the activity of the notary seems to be legitimate for the same reason that the acts of the bishop are legal.[70]

The competency of the judicial notary in an exempt clerical community is limited to causes arising from and relating to that

---

[64] Canon 374, § 2.

[65] Reiffenstuel, *Ius Canonicum Universum*, lib. II, tit. 22, *de fide instrumentorum*, n. 262.

[66] Lega and Bartoccetti, *Commentarius*, I, 153.

[67] C. 2, *de constitutionibus*, I, 2 in VI°.

[68] *Commentarius*, I, 153, footnote 2, from Pirhing, *Ius Canonicum*, lib. II,

community.[61] Territorial competency seems not to enter as a factor in any way involving the trial since the competency of the superior on which that of the notary depends is an essentially and exclusively personal one.

Should the judicial notary exceed the tenor of his appointment or the scope of his powers, the papers drawn up by him, the judicial acts, would not have the value of public documents, inasmuch as such acts would of their very nature be invalid.

Article V. Suspicion, Substitution, Resignation, Dismissal

A. The Exception of Suspicion

The names of the judges, of the auditor, and of the members of the court, including the judicial notary, should be communicated without delay to the parties in a cause so that they may be enabled to lodge objections, if circumstances warrant this. If there is any substitution of the officials, the same procedure should be observed.[62] When the exception of suspicion is brought against the judicial notary, the *praeses* of the collegiate tribunal or the judge himself, if there be but one judge, investigates the charge.[63]

Exceptions of suspicion should be presented and reviewed before the joining of issue in a cause, unless these arise only afterward or the party affirms on oath that only subsequently did he become aware of the condition. If a person wishes to enter the exception of suspicion after the cause is under way, such a party must prove to the satisfaction of the court that there was neither fraud nor malice in his delay to take action.[64]

---

tit. 22, *de fide instrumentorum*, n. 8; Roberti, *De Processibus*, I, n. 117. p. 304. footnote 4.

[59] *Commentarius*, I, 153, nn. 1 and 2.

[60] *De Processibus*, I, n. 117.

[61] Canon 503.

[62] Instruction *Provida* of the S. C. of the Sacraments, 1936, art. 26—*AAS*, XXVIII (1936), 319. In its entirety this Instruction covers pp. 313-361 of this volume of the *AAS*.

[63] Canon 1614, § 3.

[64] Canon 1628, § 1.

B. Substitution

Only the bishop, it appears, can appoint a substitute judicial notary.[65] Death, ill health, change of position, incompatible assignments, etc., may be reasons that make substitution advisable or necessary. As in other instances of substitution, the fact of the substitution should always be mentioned in the acts of the cause in order that any and all difficulties or misunderstandings may effectively be forestalled.

The assistant named by the presiding judge to the judicial notary according to the provision of Article 19, § 3, of the *Instruction of 1936* is not a substitute notary, but merely an assistant to the judicial notary. This distinction must be kept in mind.

In the process of a dispensation *super rato et non-consummato*, the *defensor vinculi* must be consulted before an assistant is assigned to the judicial notary.[66] The *Instruction of 1936* makes it clear that such consultation is not required in similar circumstances when the diocesan curia is conducting a process on the alleged nullity of a marriage.[67] The assistant provides help in the writing of the acts, in making transcripts, and in preparing documents.[68] He takes the oath of office and also the oath of observing secrecy.[69]

Although it may be argued that the judge is free in his designation of *anyone* to the office of assistant,[70] it is the opinion of this writer that the judge must limit his selection to one of the lawfully appointed judicial notaries. The terms of the *Instruction of 1936*, "*assignare*"

---

[65] Instruction *Provida* of the S. C. of the Sacraments, 1936, art. 19 § 1—*AAS*, XXVIII (1936), 318. Hereafter this Instruction will be cited as the *Instruction of 1936*.

[66] Decree of the S. C. of the Sacraments, May 17, 1923, number 32—*AAS*, XV (1923), 398-399. Hereafter, this Decree will be cited as the *Decree of 1923*. This decree along with the appended formularies covers pp. 389-436 in this volume of the *AAS*.

[67] Art. 19, § 3. The *Instruction of 1936* is divided into articles, the Decree of 1923, into numbers. It is in this same fashion that reference will be made to these two documents.

[68] Art. 19, § 3; number 32.

[69] Number 32.

[70] Doheny (*Practical Manual for Marriage Cases*, p. 128) states that the judge can *appoint* assistants, while substitutes can be appointed only by the bishop.

and "*designare*", point to such an interpretation. This *Instruction* empowers the *praeses* alone to designate ("*potest designare*") an assistant notary. If the assistant is to be of any real value beyond the doing of work that is of a purely clerical nature, he will probably be called upon to sign and attest acts, identifying himself as the assistant judicial notary. If he is to give public form to these, he must have been appointed a notary first of all. In practice, unless the judge can also appoint a judicial notary, he should limit his designation of assistant judicial notaries to such as have been lawfully appointed as judicial notaries.

C. Resignation

The judicial notary may resign for a just cause.[71] The resignation should be tendered in writing, or orally before two witnesses.[72] A record should be preserved. The resignation to be valid needs to be accepted by the one who made the appointment, by his successor, or by his superior, each of whom should not accept the resignation except for a just and proportionate cause.[73] The office does not become vacant until notice of the approval of the resignation has been received by the one who resigned.[74] All this is based on canons used by anology, since the judicial notary has no office in the strict sense.

D. Dismissal

All notaries can be removed or suspended by the one who appointed them, by his successor, or by his superior.[75] Suspension is here to be taken, according to Augustine, as temporary cessation, not as an ecclesiastical censure.[76] Lega and Bartocetti affirm that the canon comprehends an administrative and not penal procedure.[77]

---

[71] Canon 184.

[72] Canon 186.

[73] Canons 187, 189.

[74] Canon 190.

[75] Canon 373, § 5.

[76] *A Commentary on the New Code of Canon Law,* II, 408, footnote. Cf. canon 2406 for penal sanction.

[77] *Commentarius,* I, n. 151.

Removal from office implies a permanent effect. Suspension from office is of a temporary nature. Causes for suspension could be sickness, temporary press of other work, etc.

The superior of the appointee can remove a notary. Is the metropolitan capable of removing a notary of one of his suffragans? Lega and Bartoccetti believe that he can do so extrajudicially on the occasion of a canonical visitation approved by the Holy See[78] as well as judicially.[79] Augustine, on the other hand, held that the superior of the bishop in the canonical sense is the Pope and not the metropolitan, so that the latter cannot remove the notary.[80]

While Coronata feels that the vicar general could dismiss a notary, he makes such action applicable restrictively to a notary whom the vicar general had himself appointed.[81] The vicar capitular can remove or suspend a notary only with the consent of the chapter.[82]

The notary can be removed from office *ad nutum*.[83] Even though he is removable *ad nutum*, the judicial notary should enjoy some stability of office.[84]

Article VI. The Personal Qualities of a Judicial Notary

The notarial candidate must be of unblemished reputation, and rise above all suspicion.[85] While the commentators on the law before the Code of Canon Law required of the candidate, in addition to the age of puberty, some skill in canon law, Roberti says that the Code rightly places honesty and trustworthiness ahead of expertness in law.[86] The fact that skill in and knowledge of the law is nowhere explicitly mentioned in the Code does not imply that such ability and talent are of little import for a judicial notary. It should not be the practice to appoint just anybody. A judicial notary well

---

[78] Canon 274, n. 5.

[79] Canon 274, n. 7.

[80] *A Commentary of the New Code of Canon Law*, II, 408.

[81] *Institutiones*, I, n. 426, footnote 7.

[82] Canon 373, § 5.

[83] Wernz-Vidal, *Ius Canonicum*, (Vol. II, 2. ed., a P. Aguirre recognita, Romae: apud aedes Universitates Gregorianae, 1943, II, 108.

[84] Roberti, *De Processibus*, I, n. 118.

[85] Canon 373, § 4.

[86] *De Processibus*, I, n. 118, footnote 2.

versed in the norms of procedural law especially will prove of inestimable help in any process.

The Code desires that the notary be a cleric. The provision of canon 139, § 2, prohibits only the functioning of clerics as public notaries in affairs that do not involve the diocesan curia. A layman may be appointed. A lay judicial notary is expressly permitted in the process of a ratified, non-consummated marriage.[87] Such permission is implied in causes concerning the alleged nullity of sacred ordination.[88] In the criminal trial of a cleric, however, the judicial notary must be a priest.[89]

The substitution of two witnesses for the judicial notary is no longer valid. Thus there is abrogated the decretal law by which the presence of two witnesses could supply for the presence of the judicial notary.[90] Still in the Code two witnesses can supply for the presence of a public notary in a number of specifically mentioned instances.[91]

The judicial notary is forbidden to accept any presents on the occasion of a trial.[92] The term "presents" (*munera*) is very general and includes not only gifts of personal or real property, but also all services and favors.[93] Probably, the gifts of food and drink are not forbidden. They are not to be considered as *munera.* Since the Code forbids the acceptance of *munera,* it seems that the notary would not be under obligation to decline the offered food or drink.[94]

---

[87] *Decree of 1923,* number 24, § 2—*AAS,* XV (1923), 397.

[88] *Regulae Servandae in Processibus super Nullitate Sacrae Ordinationis,* 9 iun. 1931, n. 15, 2—*AAS,* XXIII (1931), 461. This decree along with the appended formularies covers pp. 457-492 in this volume of the *AAS.*

[89] Canon 373, 3.

[90] Roberti, *De Processibus,* I, n. 117, p. 304, footnote 2; Coronata, *Institutiones,* III, n. 1123; Doheny, *Canonical Procedure in Matrimonial Cases,* II, *Informal Procedure* (Milwaukee; Bruce Publishing Co., 1944), II, 142 (hereafter cited *Informal Procedure*), Wernz-Vidal (*Ius Canonicum,* VI, 103, footnote 49) seem to hold the contrary opinion.

[91] Cf. canons 1659, § 2; 2143, § 1; 2225; 2309, § 1.

[92] Canon 1624.

[93] Michael Lega, *Praelectiones in Textum Iuris Canonici de Iudiciis Ecclesiasticis* (4 vols., Romae, 1896-1901), I, 83.

[94] Woywod, S., and Smith, C., *A Practical Commentary on the Code of*

Augustine held to the contrary view that such gifts of food and drink are also to be included under the prohibition of canon 1624.[85] It would seem that the quantity of food and drink is a determining factor also.

A judicial notary who would presume to violate the law of secrecy, or to communicate to others the secret proceedings in any manner, may be punished with fines or other penalties, even with deprivation of office, in due proportion to the gravity of his guilt; and if particular laws prescribe graver penalties in any case, these laws remain in force. He may also be punished by the judge.[86]

Canon Law (2 vols., revised and enlarged edition, New York: Joseph Wagner, 1948), II, p. 247.

[85] *A Commentary on the New Code of Canon Law*, VII, 71.

[86] Canon 1625, § § 2 and 3. Cf. also canon 2406.

CHAPTER V

THE CONSTRUCTION OF THE JUDICIAL ACTS

All judicial acts are public ecclesiastical documents.[1] A public document is one composed by an official in his official capacity with due observance of the prescribed formalities, or at least in official style.[2] The fact that it can be recognized as a public document necessarily demands that it be drawn up in authentic form by a public person.[3] By "authentic" there is signified the fact that the legal form in the execution of a document was duly observed.[4] Since the judicial notary is considered in canon law a *testis qualificatus,* whose writing or signature merits public faith, all documents properly drawn up by him according to the tenor of his appointment have the value of public ecclesiastical documents.[5]

Ecclesiastical judicial acts are the records of an ecclesiastical process. These court records should be kept so exactly and in such detail that the meaning of every item and of every step in a process is clear.[6] The Code of Canon Law distinguishes the "*acta causae*" which are concerned with the merits of the cause as such, from the "*acta processus*" which pertain to the form of procedure in the trial.[7]

---

[1] Canon 1813, § 1, n. 3.

[2] Augustine, *A Commentary on the New Code of Canon Law,* VII, 254.

[3] Robert A. Willett, *The Probative Value of Documents in. Ecclesiastical Trials,* The Catholic University of American Canon Law Studies, n. 171 (Washington, D. C.: The Catholic University of America Press, 1942), p. 63.

[4] Augustine, *A Commentary on the New Code of Canon Law,* VII, 255.

[5] Canons 373, § 1; 1585, § 1; 1813, § 1, nn. 2 and 3.

[6] "*Quod non est in actis, non est in mundo.*"

[7] Canon 1642, § 1. Vaughan has suggested the following division: "The '*acta causae*' may include the *libellus;* the minutes of the sessions; documents pertinent to proofs; testimonies of parties, witnesses and experts; character testimonials and affidavits; completed commissions; procedural acts on exceptions pertinent to the cause and on incidental questions; decrees pertinent to the cause such as on the joinder of issue; briefs, animadversions and rebuttals of advocates and defenders; summations by the *ponens;* the sentence.

In the forwarding of a cause to the court of appeal, all the judicial acts of the trial are to be included in the packet that is remitted.[8]

ARTICLE I. THE PRESENCE AND SIGNATURE OF THE JUDICIAL NOTARY

It is not necessary that the judicial notary should write up all the acts in his own hand. Where court stenographers are employed these should be under the supervision of the judicial notary. They in no way supply the presence of the judicial notary, who must be on hand for all sessions at all times. The forms, questionnaires, etc., could be prepared before the sessions.[9] The use of a typewriter to compose the acts is certainly permissible.[10] The judicial notary must personally sign the acts, however. A rubber stamp or the typing in of his signature is not admissible for the required subscription.[11]

Each and every page making up the process requires the signature of the judicial notary, who also sees to it, if no secretary of the court has been appointed, that the other requirements of the law, i.e., dating, pagination, and the application of the seal of the tribunal, have been fulfilled.[12] Moreover, whenever the individual acts have been completed, or even interrupted, the judicial notary must so state and sign them, together with the judge or the *praeses,* and the others required by law.[13]

The '*acta processus*' may include memoranda of the non-judicial consulting officer; decrees appointing and changing '*turnus*' members; mandates of procurators, advocates, auditors, guardians and '*tutores;*' proofs of the dates of the process such as return receipts of registered citations, envelopes of refused or undelivered citations; citations; notifications; signed oaths; '*articuli*' or '*positiones*' of parties; letters not pertinent to the cause such as those introducing individuals, informing parties of court personnel, releasing from professional secrecy, expressing appreciation, etc.; decrees not pertinent to the decision on the cause, for example, for the *conclusio in causa* and the publication of the acts; all decrees and records on finances, etc. This division presupposes very complete minutes for each session."—*Constitutions for Diocesan Courts,* pp. 71-72, footnote 36.

[8] Decision of the Pontificial Commission for the Authentic Interpretation of the Code, 31 ian. 1942,—*AAS,* XXXIV (1942), 50.

[9] Coronata, *Institutiones,* III, n. 1123.

[10] Coronata, *loc. cit.;* Augustine, *A Comentary on the New Code of Canon Law,* VII, 40.

[11] Coronata, *loc. cit.;* Augustine, *loc. cit.*

[12] Canon 1643, §1.

[13] Canon 1643, §2.

The judicial notary should always sign the acts in the last place, thus testifying to the authenticity of the other signatures that have been appended. The other members of the court, according to the diversity of the acts, sign in the order of precedence, with an indication of the office they hold. To have any or all signatures placed on a blank sheet of paper instead of on the pages of the acts which, for one reason or another, may not be ready or completed before the court adjourns, is an abuse. It is hard to see how such a procedure could be justified. The act, and not a blank sheet of paper, is to be signed.[14]

ARTICLE 2. THE SEAL OF THE TRIBUNAL

While the signature and the presence of the judicial notary are absolutely required for the validity of the acts of a trial, the application of the seal of the tribunal does not seem to be required for the validity of the acts.[15] The absence of the seal on the act, however, can give rise to the suspicion concerning the authenticity of such an act.[16] If no special tribunal seal is available, the seal of the diocesan curia could be used.[17]

The essential element for a public document, according to Coronata, seems to be the signature of a notary or of any other public person appointed for this purpose.[18] The other conditions noted in the Code—the seal, the date and place of issuance—seem not to be necessary for validity, but constitute an integral part of the act. The definition of authenticity may be enlarged upon here to signify the external marks of attestation made by a competent person that a certain writing was drawn up in all its parts by him to whom it is attributed.[19] The seal is one of these external marks of attestation.

[14] Canon 1780, § 2: "*Denique actui subscribere debent testis, iudex et notarius.*"

[15] "Nullitas actus autem sequi videtur tantum ex defectu subscriptionis illius qui actum posuit et notarii"—Roberti, *De Processibus,* I, n. 188; F. Cappello, *Praxis Processualis* (Taurini-Romae: Marietti, 1940), n. 11.

[16] Roberti, *De Processibus,* I, n. 188. Cf. *Instruction of 1936,* art. 159, § 2; Doheny, *Formal Procedure,* p. 403.

[17] Cappello, *Praxis Processualis,* n. 12.

[18] *Institutiones,* III, n. 1341. Cf. canon 1813.

[19] Willett, *The Probative Value of Documents in Ecclesiastical Trails,* p. 63.

The purpose of these solemnities is to prevent forgery and to aid the judge in deciding whether the document in question is or is not genuine. Consequently, they are to be considered as a means to an end, rather than as an end in themselves.

According to Ferraris, the use of the seal was not required for the substance of an act (except in wills, privileges and the like, where the seal is of the substance of an act), but only for easier proof of authenticity of such an act. The seal was a kind of confirmation of those things which were contained in writing.[20] Reiffenstuel noted that for the most part it was customary to add the seal not because it regularly was necessary or required for the substance of an act (as in the case of wills, privileges, and the like), but for easier proof, "*nam sigillans scripturam contenta in ea praesupponit vera et videtur fateri omnia contenta in ipsa.*"[21] The seal was always added *ad cautelam* when the *instrumentum* was public.[22] Paul Fournier (1855-1935) discovered that around the thirteenth century an act prepared and drawn up by a notary was carried to the sealer, who gave it authentic form by applying the seal of the court. At Reims, every act had to have the seal affixed within two months of its date, under pain of nullity.[23]

The use of the official seal offers the most common means of determining that the writer was acting in his official capacity.[24] It is the opinion of Lega and Bartoccetti that the seal should always be added, even though the applying of the seal is not specifically intimated: it is for the purpose of authenticating the signature of the judicial notary and the judge.[25]

It seems that the following conclusion may be maintained: that

---

[20] *Bibliotheca,* VII, s.v. *Sigillum,* n. 19; in n. 33, however, *in manu aliena* there is added: "An ad validitatem instrumenti a notario confecti requiratur sigillum ipsius? Praevaluit opinio affirmativa."

[21] *Ius Canonicum Universum,* lib. II, tit. 22, "*de fide instrumentorum,*" n. 99.

[22] *Ibid.,* n. 98.

[23] 'L'acte dresse par le notaire etait porte au scelleur, qui lui donnait la forme authentique en y apposant le sceau de la cour. A Reims, tout acte devait etre presente au sceau dans les deux mois de sa date, sous peine de nullite,"—*Les Officialites au Moyan Age,* p. 51.

[24] Willett, *The Probative Value of Documents in Ecclesiastical Trials,* p. 50.

[25] *Commentarius,* I, 288.

for a valid judicial act, the signature of the judicial notary is a *sine qua non*, an essential part of an act, while the seal of the court, although not an essential part, is an integral part of such an act.

According to canon 1894, n. 1, the sentence is vitiated with a remedial nullity if the the lawful citation was lacking. This is considered by some authors to be the citation introducing the cause.[26] If the parties appear of their own accord, there is no need of a citation. In regard to the other defects as well as that of the seal mentioned in canon 1894, when the defect has been supplied, the sentence becomes validated and is to be published.[27]

Lemieux seems to indicate that canon 1894, n. 1, refers to the citation required in the formal pronouncing of the sentence according to canon 1877. He claims that the opinion of Roberti, Coronata and Noval, who regard canon 1894 as referring to the citation connected with the introducing of the cause, would make it necessary to classify the defect appropriately as an irremediable one, since with such a defect there would be no need or chance to remedy the sentence, since all the acts of the cause would be null and there could be no sentence.[28] Accordingly, solely the defect of the citation which is required by canon 1877 could come under the terms of canon 1894, i.e., emerges as a remediable defect.[29]

The citation of the parties introducing the cause is, then, the citation that is treated in canon 1715. All the requirements set up by the canon are necessary for a valid citation, and indeed for the acts of the process.[30]

Is one to regard the requirement of the seal on the citation as an essential requisite for the validity of the citation, despite the general assumption that the absence of the seal does not affect the validity of any of the judicial acts of a trial? Here again, so it seems to the writer, the seal is required simply *ad integritatem*, although this

---

[26] Roberti, *De Processibus*, II, n. 489; Coronata, *Institutiones*, III, n. 1418; Noval, *De Iudiciis*, n. 661, p. 437.

[27] Delisle Lemieux, *The Sentence in Ecclesiastical Procedure*, The Catholic University of America Canon Law Studies, n. 187 (Washington, D. C.: The Catholic University of America, 1934), p. 99.

[28] Lemieux, *op. cit.*, p. 98.

[29] Lemieux, *loc. cit.*

[30] Canon 1723.

is not undisputed. Vermeersch-Cruesen expressly demand the seal of the court on the *scheda citatoria "ut citatio valeat."*[31]

On the other hand, the use of the ablative construction points to a modal condition that pertains to an integral part of the citation, and not to an essential part. According to Lega and Bartoccetti, canon 1723 demands for validity only the "*praescriptiones quoad substantiam*" of canon 1715, and seal is not one of these.[32] In commenting on the *Decree of 1923* Doheny expressly states that "the fixing of the seal is not required for the validity of the document."[33]

When the testimony is gathered in the manner provided for by canon 1770, § 2, n. 4, it seems desirable that the delegated priest affix the parish seal before returning the recorded testimony to the chancery office or diocesan tribunal. The authenticity for the written statement is thus affirmed. The same procedure should be observed by any rogatory commission delegated by the court.

The seal of the court is, or at least should be, distinct from the curial seal. In the event that no tribunal seal is available, the curial seal could be substituted. The observations of Reiffenstuel, pertinent to cases where no tribunal seal is available as in the gathering of testimony by a rogatory commission, seems very practical: if no proper seal is to be had, or at least is not presently available or cannot be acquired easily, then another could be used, and the one who so acts should explain the reasons why and indicate specifically whose seal he used on this occasion.[34]

Some practical deducible conclusions are the following:

1) The court seal is an integral part, like the date and place of issue, of judicial acts.

2) The seal is an authentification of the signature of the writer,

---

[31] *Epitome Iuris Canonici* (3 vols., Vol. III, 6. ed., Mechliniae-Romae: H. Dessain, 1946), n. 146.

[32] *Commentarius,* II, 539: "Item omissio sigilli tribunalis, fere semper, nihil detrahit certitudini quae obiective habetur de authenticitate subscriptionis iudicis et notarii. Eo magis quod appositio sigilli in littera canonis § [1715], praescribitur sub ablativo; et est regula interpretationis, quae ita significantur, non facere conditionem substantialem actus."

[33] *Informl Procedure,* p. 298.

[34] *Ius Canonicum Universum,* II, tit. 22, "*de fide instrumentorum,*" n. 73.

the judicial notary and the judge and others; it is a means of dedetermining the official nature of an act or document.

3) If no seal, proper or otherwise, is available, this fact should be noted in the act.

4) The parish seal would be adequate for the testimony taken by a delegated commission according to the provisions of canon 1770, § 2, n. 4.

5) In practice, the seal of the court should always be affixed to each page of the judicial acts. Likewise, copies of the acts forwarded to the court of appeal should always bear the seal of the tribunal.

6) The judicial notary should see to it that the seal of the court is properly affixed to each page of the judiical acts.

Article 3. The Preparation of the Judicial Acts

A. Dates

Each and every act should bear on it an indication of the day, the month, and the year of its composition. This is suggested for the act, not for each and every page. An indication of the place where the act was drawn up or completed should also be added.[85]

The dating of the acts does not seem to be necessary for their validity.[86]

B. Erasures and Corrections

Should it become necessary because of error or omission to make corrections in the acts, additions, changes, or modifications, then the judicial notary should expressly note this fact.[87] Mention may be made of this on the side or at the bottom of the page where such changes are made, with the use of the form: "*Manu mea correxi* (*or* "*mutavi*" *or* "*addidi*"). *N.N. Notarius iudicialis.*"

It has also been suggested that greater discretion is exhibited when the original text is preserved whole and entire, any and all

[85] Coronata, *Institutiones*, III, n. 1164, p. 73, footnote 8.

[86] Coronata, *ibid.*, n. 1342, p. 247, footnote 4.

[87] Cappello, *Praxis Processualis*, n. 7.

modifications being added at the end. The signatures are repeated if the circumstances warrant it.[38]

C. Copies

Any notary can attest that the copy is a faithful transcription of the original record.[39] Some courts stamp each page with a rubber stamp, "*concordat cum originali*", and the notary signs each page. Vaughan ventures the opinion that "an affidavit at the beginning or at the end of each transcription attesting the faithfulness of the entire work and signed by the notary would be sufficient, especially if the transcriptions are sent directly to the court of appeals and never are in the hands of the parties. At least since the second and third copies are duplicates of the first, the stamp and signature, if placed on each page, need be on only the first copy." [40] Augustine seemed to regard a single attestation as sufficient.[41] Coronata requires that the copy be signed and sealed like the original.[42]

In practice, the judicial notary or the court secretary should see to it that each page bears the signature of the judicial notary and the seal of the court before the copy is released. In this regard it is suggested also that at least three copies be made of the original acts and forwarded to the court of appeal. In this way the court of second instance will have one copy for the *defensor vinculi,* one for the advocate, and one for the court. Such a method should expedite procedure in the appeal court.

An index of all the acts and documents should accompany the transcript.[43] For the competent judicial notary this is, of course, a simple matter, since he will have outlined and indexed the process from its very beginning.

The mandate of the judge is necessary before any notary may give out copies of any judicial acts or documents which have been acquired by reason of a process.[44]

---

[38] Roberti, *De Processibus*, I, n. 188.

[39] Canon 374, § 1, n. 3.

[40] *Constitutions for Diocesan Courts*, pp. 74, 75.

[41] *A Commentary on the New Code of Canon Law*, VII, 92.

[42] *Institutiones*, III, n. 1165.

[43] Canon 1644, § 1.

[44] Canon 1645, § 3.

The original acts are drawn up, as far as possible, in the Latin language, unless a just cause suggests otherwise; the questions submitted to and the answers given by the witnesses, along with other items of a similar nature, should be drawn up in the vernacular.[45] When judicial acts are sent to a court where the vernacular of the first court is unknown, all the acts should be translated into the Latin language, all due care having been taken that the translation is a faithful one.[46] The Sacred Congregation for the Oriental Church seems to be the only congregation of the Roman Curia which accepts cases written in English.[47] Since English has now become an almost universal language, it is to be hoped that it will in the not too distant future take its place along with the other curial languages, Latin, Italian and French.

Article 4. The Preservation of the Judicial Acts

A. The Care of the Judicial Acts

The acts form the permanent record of a process. Attention must be drawn to the necessity of using a high quality paper in preparing and making transcripts of the acts. If the acts are prepared by hand, a durable and specially prepared ink should be used. If a typewriter is employed, care should be taken that the type is clean and sharp and that the imprint derived from the ribbon be of quality ink.

Since the judicial notary will have charge of the acts during a process, he should see to it that the acts are properly preserved. It is likely that the chancery office will provide the equipment. For this purpose, durable protfolios and filing cabinets are very serviceable. Bulkiness is a problem that often arises as a process unfolds. It is suggested that hanging folders, the type that can be suspended in the filing cabinet, will aid in meeting this situation. While it is obvious that not all the original acts and documents will be made up of papers of the same size, the use, wherever possible of a uniform size—standard or legal—will make for orderliness. The copies or transcriptions can and should be made on paper that is uniform

[45] Canon 1642, § 2.
[46] Canon 1644, § 2.
[47] *AAS*, XXVII (1935), 340, n. 28.

in size. The use of onionskin paper is a safeguard against bulkiness, but it is believed that a paper just as thin without being so transparent will prove easier to read for those whose duty requires a close reading and inspection of the acts.

B. The Recording of the Testimony

In order to expedite the sessions that make up a process, some courts have the judicial notary make all entries in longhand. In other instances the judicial notary types the testimony directly as it is given, or takes it down in stenography. In some cases stenographers are employed by the court, a method which is not inexpensive. The actual method of taking testimony in ecclesiastical trials is nowhere specified in the Code; no special system for court reporting has been designated. What is important is that the transcription be accurate and complete.

The use of a dictaphone to record testimony seems to be one of the more adequate and satisfactory methods in court procedure. It is a sound recording. Not one word is lost. It records items that a judicial notary might overlook. A verbatim account is sometimes invaluable. The recorded testimony is played back to the witness before he leaves the court room, thus giving him a chance, as required by law, to add, correct, change or modify what he has said. The testimony, recorded on a cylinder, is run off again and typed up soon after the session; it is then ready for the required signatures. Before the witness leaves the court room, he should certify that he approves of his recorded deposition. When the act is ready, he returns to the court to affix his signature, or if circumstances make this impossible, then a notary dispatched by the court should obtain his required signature to the testimony. The witness should read the written deposition before signing the document.

A wire recording machine may also be used, but this method does not seem to lend itself to the accuracy of the dictaphone cylinder, which is marked and can be played back at any point.

Doheny requires that the transcript of the testimony be ready for a reading and for the affixing of the signatures before the witness leaves the tribunal. Thus he interprets the provision of the law in a strict manner.[48] In view of the manifest merits of the dictaphone method, wherein all the provisions of the law are complied with, it seems that, when the witness has approved his testimony as recorded, the signature of the witness, could be obtained later without serious prejudice to the provisions of the law, as long as it were duly authenticated by the notary. At least one large mid-western archdiocese is employing this procedure, and with signal success. The description above has been based on the present writer's personal observations at that tribunal.

Article V. The Judicial Notary as Court Reporter

It is the duty of the judicial notary to assist at the examination of the parties, the witnesses and the experts, and to record in writing all that transpires in the sessions of the tribunal.

The Code of Canon Law specifies that not only the substance, but the very words of the testimony are to be taken down, unless the judge directs that only the substance needs to be recorded. It is for the judge, and not the judicial notary, to decide the course of action.[49] If the words themselves cannot be recorded, either because they were given too fast, or because they were incoherent and not logically interrelated, the judge will dictate the reply that is to be recorded in the acts.[50]

The judicial notary need not repeat the questions already written up, but will merely number the replies with the same enumeration with which the corresponding questions were numbered.[51] To give the judicial notary at the beginning of each session a copy of questions to be asked will be a real help in expediting the recording of the testimony

Two extremes to be avoided in court reporting have been singled out: the excessively diffuse report, and especially the exaggeratedly brief one. The "yes" and "no" answer type has been the target of special criticism.[52]

---

[48] *Formal Procedure*, p. 321.

[49] Canon 1778.

[50] *Decree of 1923*, number 44, § 2.

[51] *Ibid.*, § 3.

[52] *Instruction of 1936*, art. 129.

When the witness is too "talkative," the judge may dictate a summary of the reply to the judicial notary. The judge has this discretionary power to rearrange and organize the statements made by the witnesses. [63] The reprobated monosylabic reply as recorded in the judicial acts often results from the inefficiently performed work of the judicial notary, rather than from the terse manner in which the witness rendered his replies.

Both the judge and the judicial notary should take great care to see that the meaning and thought of the person are clearly indicated in his recorded reply to a question. While the substance of a reply may seem to the judicial notary to resolve itself to a yes or no answer at times, words that at the moment seem negligible may assume importance and be of great value later in the process. The Roman Rota has itself condemned the absolutely unfair and careless abridgement of answers into a series of monosyllabic replies.[64] Since each question in a well-prepared interrogatory has a definite purpose, even though the question be repeated, the repetition and answer may bring up new points and new shades of meaning. Hence, for a judicial notary to disregard the rephrased answer, and simply to record "Answered above" or See above", would be gross negligence of duty.

What the Code of Canon Law merely indicates in regard to the person who can request verbatim reports[65] the *Instruction of 1936* [66] has stated explicitly. Accordingly, not only the judge (mentioned in the Code), but also the one who hears the testimony and the depositions, as also the party, the witness and the expert can insist on a verbatim record of the given testimony. The party, the witness and the expert are not obliged to sign the deposition until the verbatim testimony has been recorded as requested.

The reading back of the testimony is usually done by the judicial notary. This may be done by anyone, however. If the judicial notary does not personally read back the testimony, he should be

---

[63] Canon 1778; *Instruction of 1936*, art. 103, § 2.

[64] *Sacrae Romanae Rotae Decisiones seu Sententiae quae prodierunt ab anno* 1909—(Romae: Typis Polyglottis Vaticanis, 1912—), XIX (1927), 481.

[65] Canons 1778, 1780.

[66] Article103, § 2.

present at the rereading so that he can attest that the rights of the party, of the witness or of the expert have been safeguarded. The practice of having a witness sign a blank sheet of paper because the testimony is not yet it its final form, and of then having this appended later when everything has been typed out or written up, is an abuse that no court may countenance.

The judicial notary should mention in the acts whether the oath was taken, dispensed with, or refused, whether the parties and any other persons were present, what questions were added "*ex officio,*" and generally anything worthy of note that happened while the examination was being conducted.[57]

a) Since there is a difference in the evaluation of testimony given under oath or without oath, the reason for a special annotation is apparent. Special mention should be made of a refusal to take the oath by anyone, whether it be on the grounds of religious convictions against oaths, whether it be in view of atheistic and communistic principles, or the like.

b) The names of all present during a session should be noted in the acts, the judges, day, place, who was admitted to assist at the session.

c) The *ex officio* submitted questions should be so identified,[58] as well as the source of these. Such questions make more sense when asked and recorded in the proper order of questioning than when all the *ex officio* invoked queries are made at the end of the prepared interrogatory. The enumeration of the questions should be interrupted, the *ex officio* raised questions should there be inserted, and then the enumeration should be resumed. It will be helpful to indicate the sources of the *ex officio* raised questions by annotating them "*ex off. iud.*", or "*ex officio def. vinc.*", etc.

d) If written documents are used, the tenor of these should be indicated in the acts when the documents are produced in a session. Such documents should be inserted among the judicial acts unless they already form part of the deposition in the acts, and then it will suffice to report in the acts which part of the document was read

---

[57] Canon 1779.

[58] Canon 1742, 1; *Instruction of 1936*, art. 101.

by the witness.[59] The documents that are deposited in the chancery of the tribunal are to be safeguarded by the judicial notary, who sees to it that the documents remain in the chancery and are examined there by the parties, the *defensor vinculi*, and even by the judges themselves. The judicial notary is responsible for the documents, hence he should be most insistent on this point.[60]

e) It has been suggested that the judicial notary will know from experience what matters are worthy of note in a process.[61] Such comment is of little help to a judicial notary who, intent upon a faithful discharge of the duties which his new appointment has laid on him, is confronted with the prescription of canon law that he is to note in the acts everything worth remembering. It must be deduced that the legislator presumes that the judicial notary has received some training in judicial procedure. In the allotting of this discretionary power a rather thorough grasp of procedural law seems to be taken for granted. The really competent judicial notary will be constantly watchful, and his acts will bear witness to his integrity and faithfulness in the service of truth: his acts will record and contain every pertinent detail with such clarity that even the court of appeal will have a complete understanding of every situation and point in the trial, to say nothing of the help afforded the members of his own court in view of his conscientious attention to his duties. The judge may direct the judicial notary in this important work.

The judicial notary, *ex suo officio*, notes what is worthy of memory; he makes these notations not merely at the command of the judge. Such memoranda seem to be left solely to the discretion of the judicial notary. When a judge decides that a certain point should be noted, however, the judicial notary is advised to make such notations, even though to him a particular circumstance does not seem to be worth mentioning. Practice will dictate the manner of proceeding that the judicial notary will pursue so that the demands of the truth and the claims of his dignity are both properly respected. When he writes up the acts he refers to whatever was required by

[59] Lega and Bartoccetti, *Commentarius*, II, 718.

[60] *Instruction of 1936*, article 161; canons 1819, 1820.

[61] Doheny, *Informal Procedure*, p. 330.

the judge, adding the annotation that "these have been noted at the instance of the judge." [62]

The judicial notary, of course, has absolutely no right to propose any questions, directly or indirectly. Should he discover that some question has not been fully answered, or that the answer to some part of a multiple question be omitted, it would certainly not be out of place for him to bring the matter to the attention of the judge or the auditor in a discreet manner. He might even point out privately a pertinent point of law to the *defensor vinculi* or other proper official. Naturally, he should exercise a great amount of prudence and caution in such matters. On the other hand, such proffered help should not be brushed aside or taken amiss by the official so advised.

It is quite apparent from all this that a competent and experienced judicial notary is of inestimable help in the smooth functioning of a diocesan tribunal. The thoughtless assertion that "anybody can be a judicial notary" proves false at every test.

The formal excellence of the judicial acts is assured by the efficient excellence of the judicial notary.

---

[62] Lega and Bartoccetti, *Commentarius*, II, 718.

CHAPTER VI

THE ROLE OF THE JUDICIAL NOTARY

ARTICLE I. THE GENERAL DUTIES OF THE JUDICIAL NOTARY

In order to fill out the description of the judicial notary, one must discuss the role of the judicial notary in the ecclesiastical process itself. The functions of the judicial notary have already been mentioned and discussed for the most part, since the office and duties of the judicial notary are so closely related. The general duties of the notary will be treated in almost summary form in this first section of the present chapter, while some of the salient features of his position at various stages of the trial will receive consideration in the rest of the chapter.

The general duties of the judicial notary may be listed as the following:

1) To be present at all the sessions of a process, and to draw up or at least to sign all the acts, both those which regard the merits of the case and those which regard the form of procedure;[1]

2) to see to it that all the acts are written up;[2] and indeed in the Latin language as far as that is possible, as long as there is not a just cause for doing otherwise; the questions submitted to and the answers given by the witnesses, and also other items of a similar nature, are written in the vernacular;[3]

3) to number, sign and apply the seal of the tribunal to each page of the process;[4]

4) to gather and preserve all the acts carefully, properly and conscientiously.[5]

---

[1] Canon 1585.

[2] Canon 1642, § 1.

[3] Canon 1642, § 2.

[4] Canon 1643, § 1.

[5] *Instruction of 1936*, art. 73.

[6] Canon 1645, § 3; *Instruction of 1936*, art. 73.

5) to take precautions lest the acts, and especially the ones that are to be kept secret, fall into the hands of outsiders;[6]

6) to attest all documents.[7]

7) to arrange properly the protocol or the register of the causes heard by the court;[8]

8) to record completely and faithfully everything whatsoever of judicial value that transpires during each session.

It may seem that the foregoing list is far from complete. It could of course be expanded. But it may prove adequate at least as a general guide. To insert many detailed items would be repetitious. These have already been treated, or due consideration will be given to them in the remainder of this study.

Article II. Some Salient Features of the Role of the Judicial Notary at Various Stages of a Judicial Process

A. In the Introductory Stage

The judicial notary is present when the complaint which serves to introduce a cause in court is proposed orally. He draws up the submitted complaint in written form, to be read and approved by the petitioner.[9]

If the judicial notary draws up the bill of complaint, it is not required that he do so in the presence of the judge.[10] Such a bill of complaint should contain mention of the mandate of the judge and of the approval of the petitioner. The petitioner's approval of the text of the document should be recorded in the judicial acts as drawn up by the notary. It is important that these matters be incorporated in the bill of complaint signed by the plaintiff. The bill of complaint will be the basis for the joinder of issue, and may not be changed upon the joinder of issue unless circumstances warrant. The judicial notary in such an instance could be charged with the drawing up of a faulty bill of complaint if he had not

[7] Canon 1813, § 1, n. 2; *Instruction of 1936*, art. 73.

[8] *Instruction of 1936*, art. 73.

[9] Canon 1707.

[10] Lega and Bartoccetti, *Commentarius*, II, 514.

explicitly mentioned the plaintiff's approval of the formulation of the complaint in the bill of complaint. For the notary to allege that he was not compelled to mention the fact that approval was given, according to canon 1717, § 3, is no excuse. By his office he is bound to set down faithfully and reliably in writing whatever is of rightful interest to the court and to give his attestation for it.

The judicial notary likewise records the orally signified appointment of the procurator. If the one who has issued the mandate does not know how to write, mention of this is to be made in the acts, and the judicial notary may sign the mandate in place of this person.[11] He notes the address where the plaintiff or his procurator wish to receive the communications of the court.[12] He likewise incorporates mention of the appointment of the advocate.[13]

The judicial notary is to be present whenever there is need of the administration of an oath at any stage of the trial.[14] He is not empowered in virtue of his office to administer the oath to the parties, the witnesses or the experts. However, he may be given general delegation for this by any member of the court who is authorized in law to administer the oath.[15]

He signs all the decrees of citation and notification, and affixes the seal of the tribunal to these.[16] If the parties litigant appear of their own accord, there is no need of a citation. In such a case the judicial notary notes in the acts that the parties were present of their own accord.[17]

He is present at the joinder of issue (*contestatio litis*), though no solemnities are required for such an action.[18] For causes wherein it has proved difficult to obtain the co-operation of the respondents, Vaughan describes a system for the gathering of the desired information by a priest notary who functions successively as a messenger

[11] Canon 1659, 2.
[12] Canon 1708.
[13] Canon 1661.
[14] Canons 1621, 1622, 1623; *Instruction of 1936*, art. 73.
[15] Doheny, *Formal Procedure*, p. 235.
[16] Canon 1715, § 2.
[17] Canon 1711, § 2.
[18] Canon 1727.

of the court, as a judicial notary, and as a procurator for the party.[19] Such a procedure is unusual. It could be used only when ordinary methods have failed, in order to obviate a declaration of contumacy on the part of the respondent. Note is made of it here because of the possible role of the notary in such a procedure.

B. During the Process of the Trial

Since much of the material that might be included here has been dealt with previously, the following two points alone have been singled out for comment at this point.

The judicial notary records the report of the experts who may have been called for service in the trial. If the report is given orally, the judicial notary takes it down in writing immediately and the report is then signed by both the expert and the judicial notary.[20] If the expert makes a written report, the judicial notary is present at its presentation to the court, and attests by his singature the authenticity of the report.

There have been and there will be hearings of causes which require a personal and local inspection. The judicial notary keeps a careful record of the day and the hour when the inspection was held, stating who was present and what was said and done at the inspection, and what was decreed by the judge.[21] This record must be signed by the judge—or the auditor or delegated judge who made the actual inspection, although the Code does not explicitly mention these—and the judicial notary.[22] The judicial inspection, like the comparison of the copy of a document with the original, could probably be undertaken by the notary himself in view of the nature of the particular action to be performed.[23]

C. In the Concluding Stage

At the final pleading of a cause the Code requires that one of the notaries of the tribunal be present in order that, if the judge demands

[19] *Constitutions for Diocesan Courts*, p. 80.
[20] Canon 1801, § 1.
[21] Canon 1811, § 1.
[22] Canon 1811, § 2.
[23] Canon 374, § 1, 3°; canon 1821.

it, or a party asks for it and the judge consents, he may immediately make a report of the discussion, the confessions, or the conclusions.[24] While the Code does not specify a particular notary, but simply one of the notaries of the tribunal, the *Instruction of 1936* definitely assigns this duty to the actuary who has been appointed to serve in the cause at trial. Any judicial notary, so it seems, can qualify for this designation, but if one may regard the *Instruction of 1936* as being interpretative of the Code with reference to other as well as matrimonial causes, *servatis servandis*,[25] then the notary of the tribunal should be the designated judicial notary for the entire cause. It seems, however, that any judicial notary could perform this function, having made mention of his identity in the acts themselves, since the essential element of the law, namely the presence of a judicial notary, would be fulfilled.

The judicial notary of the cause is excluded from the meeting of the judges of the collegiate tribunal for the discussion preliminary to the formulating of the sentence. In this regard Metz indicates that "in all causes which of necessity must be tried before a diocesan collegiate tribunal, only the judges are to be admitted to the meeting during which, as contemplated in the law of canon 1871, § 1, the cause will be discussed with a view toward terminating the cause by arriving at a just and equitable decision." [26]

Accordingly, "since minutes of the session will be kept, including the fact of the meeting, the names of those present, the place where and the time when held, the decision, excluding any mention of the *vota* or of the discussion, the presiding judge may be asked to designate one judge present, ordinarily the *ponens*, to record essential information lest it be lost." [27] In this regard Metz further notes that "in the event that the presiding judge has with the assent of the other judges of the tribunal taken upon himself the duties of the recording judge, then the presiding judge ought not to appoint

---

[24] Canon 1866, § 4; *Instruction of 1936*, art. 73

[25] Roberti, *De Processibus*, I, n. 108, p. 284.

[26] *The Recording Judge in the Ecclesiastical Collegiate Tribunal*, The Catholic University of America Canon Law Studies, n. 287 (Washington, D. C.: The Catholic University of America Press, 1949), p. 79; *Instruction of 1936*, art. 198.

[27] Vaughan, *Constitutions for Diocesan Courts*, p. 108.

himself as notary for the final meeting, but rather ought to assign these duties to one of the other judges of the tribunal."[28] This procedure has been noted here in some detail, inasmuch as it reflects another occasion, not of dispensing with the judicial notary, but of having someone else who performs a function that apparently is notarial in character.

The judicial notary signs the sentence,[29] and does so last of all. Since the signature of each judge on the solemn form of the sentence is proof that the sentence was submitted to the individual judge as one of the collegiate judiciary for approval, regardless of the judge's opinion, the notary should witness each signature. Doheny seems to indicate that a judicial notary is not required to witness the affixing of a judge's signature when he states that the judges may examine and sign the sentence privately and individually, and after all the judges have affixed their signatures to the sentence, the notary should sign it and then place it with the acts of the case in the files of the chancery.[30] By his own signature at the end the judicial notary attests to the genuineness of everything in the document, of the signatures, etc. The judicial notary should, therefore, be present at the signing by each judge. The court seal should be affixed, even though no specific mention is made of it, and its absence does not affect the validity of the document inasmuch as the affixing of the seal is not set as an essential requirement for the validity of the sentence.[31]

The judicial notary may inform the parties of the dispositive part of the sentence.[32] Copies of the sentence may be made according to the instructions of the *Ponens,* the presiding judge, the tribunal or the *Officialis.* The judicial notary may not show the sentence to anyone, however, without the special authorization of the same officials.[33]

---

[28] *The Recording Judge in the Ecclesiastical Collegiate Tribunal,* p. 79.

[29] Canon 1874, § 5.

[30] *Formal Procedure,* p. 483.

[31] Canon 1894.

[32] *Instruction of 1936,* art. 73.

[33] *Regulae servandae in iudiciis apud S. R. Rotae Tribunal,* 4 aug. 1910, § 188—*AAS,* II (1910), 838; Doheny, *Formal Procedure,* p. 483.

The publication of the sentence is absolutely necessary, and express mention is to be made of this in the acts in order that there may be established the duration of time that is granted for the possible invoking of an appeal.[54] The judicial notary should indicate the day, the month and the year of the notification of the sentence, and in the same acts diligently preserve the written confirmation of the receipt of the published sentence.[55]

The judicial notary, is, of course, one of the essential officials in an appeal when the party does not know how to write. When the appeal is made orally immediately after the sentence has been read publicly, the judicial notary immediately puts it down in writing.

Article III. Procedure in the Ordinary Courts of Second Instance

The judicial notary is, of course, one of the essential officials in the ordinary court of second instance. His appointment and designation are made in the same manner as in the court of first instance. His duties are the same, for the most part, as those already described. The acts of the process in the court of second instance would be invalid if the court functioned without the judicial notary.[56]

It appears that both the admission as well as the rejection of the bill of complaint is a matter for the tribunal to expedite.[57] The taking of action in this matter on the part of the tribunal postulates the attendance of the judicial notary. After the petition of appeal has been admitted by the court of second instance and the necessary citations have been served, the point in question is resolved by the joinder of issue. The judicial notary is present at this session, since the point of litigation is properly formulated now, and a record of this is inserted in the acts of the cause.[58] When the parties indicate by letter their intention to litigate, and are sufficiently informed of the

---

[54] Cf. canon 1881.

[55] Cappello, *Praxis Processualis*, n. 47.

[56] Cf. Loras Lane, *Matrimonial Procedure in the Ordinary Courts of Second Instance*, The Catholic University of America Canon Law Studies, n. 253 (Washington, D. C.: The Catholic University of America Press, 1947), p. 76.

[57] *Instruction of 1936*, art. 61.

[58] Canon 1727.

point or points at issue, this correspondence should be inserted in the acts by the judicial notary.[39]

The presence and subscription of the judicial notary are required for the validity of any of the acts of the process.[40]

Article IV. Summary Cases

The simplified procedure which canons 1990 ff. call for is of the judicial order.[41] In the conduct of such cases the judge must follow those rules which exist as essential or procedural requisites for the validity of the eventual sentence rendered by the competent judge. Summary cases are judicial trials, and so "for the validity of the process in informal trials there must be compliance with all the *essential* demands which are inherent in the conduct of a judicial trial." [42]

Before a tribunal begins an informal case the usual designation of the judicial notary should be made.[43] Since summary cases are of a judicial order, it is only fitting to speak of the one who is employed for recording the acts in the trial as the judicial notary.

In the gathering of the required testimony and in the drawing up of the acts of the cause the employment of a judicial notary will aid greatly in expediting matters. Since the process will be composed of judicial acts, it is difficult to see how the use of the judicial notary could be omitted. All acts require his signature for validity. His signature is the sign of confirmation of the authenticity of the acts. It is by his presence only that the judicial notary can attest to the testimony and proceedings in such a way that he can conscientiously append his signature for the purpose of creating public credence with reference to the acts of the trial.

Is it possible for the bishop to hear the parties in his presence alone and then afterwards dictate to the judicial notary what trans-

[39] Lane, *Matrimonial Procedure in the Ordinary Courts of Second Instance*, p. 120.

[40] Canon 1585.

[41] Comm. Pont. Intr., die 6 dec.1943—*AAS*, XXXVI (1944), 94.

[42] C. V. Bastnagel, "Testimony in Summary Cases," *The Jurist* (Washington, D. C., 1941—), V (1945), 444.

[43] Doheny, *Informal Procedure*, p. 142.

pired? Such procedure, if followed, would seem to be an abuse that should not be tolerated. Such action on the part of the bishop, would, to say the least, "imply an inequitable demand upon the notary, who by affixing his signature is held accountable with a primary responsibility for the correctness and accuracy of the recorded acts." [44]

Since the procedure in summary cases is judicial, the auditor who has been appointed to gather testimony should be distinct from the judicial notary, as in non-summary cases. The office of auditor and judicial notary are incompatible, as has been pointed out. To act otherwise and have the case heard in the presence of simply the auditor seems to be insufficient, "just as it seems not to suffice to have the bishop alone hear the parties in the absence of a notary whose name is to be affixed as a signature to the acts." [45]

The hearing of testimony in cases conducted according to the rulings of canons 1990 ff. can be delegated by the bishop, who can sanction subdelegation. If the judicial notary himself has a general delegation to hear cases, he should subdelegate to another the power of functioning as an auditor in the case and then personally function in his capacity of judicial notary. Since the notary cannot himself direct any questions, the services of an auditor are required. In the gathering of the testimony of the parties and the witnesses it is difficult to understand how the functioning of the one without at least the presence of the other can be justified.

From the time of his first official appearance in trials the *presence* of a notary was of the essence of his prescribed duties of office. By his presence the notary was to testify that all was done properly, and his preesnce was a safeguard for the person who rendered testimony in the trial. The signature of the notary is the guarantee that he was present when that transpired which the acts describe and contain. To have a judicial notary come in and sign testimony when he was not a personal witness at the taking of it is certainly against the spirit of the law, and while the signature may possibly suffice in fulfillment of the letter of the law, such action is an abuse and constitutes a morally unjustifiable practice.

[44] C. V. Bastnagel, "Testimony in Summary Cases," *The Jurist*, V (1945), 445.

[45] *Ibid.*, 446.

CHAPTER VII

THE NOTARY EMPLOYED IN NON-JUDICIAL PROCESSES

The fundamental norm concerning the notary employed as actuary is such that all ecclesiastical processes are affected by it. No distinction is made as to the particular type of process that demands such a notary.[1] The prescription extends to all processes, formal and informal. This study has as its aim and scope the consideration of only that notary who is employed as actuary in *judicial processes*. The reason for the terminology "judicial notary" becomes more evident when the various types of processes are delineated. This last chapter intends only to indicate the non-judicial processes in which a notary is employed. To refer to such a notary as the judicial notary would be misleading. It is hoped that from the ensuing commentary the true scope of the judicial notary will be all the more evident, as well as the reason for the assumption of terminology "judicial notary" with reference to judicial procedure only.

In every form of procedure the office, the rights and the duties of the notary are practically uniform. Doheny has pointed out the paramount importance of the notary in all informal proceedings: "Frequently, tribunals receive documents of one type or another about which doubts may be entertained. To clarify such dubious points, documents can be drawn up in the presence of the ecclesiastical notary, under his authority and surveillance, and thus they can have the value of public ecclesiastical documents."[2]

For all the processes mentioned in the third part of Book Four of the Code of Canon Law there is need of employing a notary for keeping the minutes of the proceedings and for signing them.[3] Vermeersch-Creusen note that the omission of the appointment of a notary does not seem to block the validity of such processes, but

[1] Canon 1585.

[2] *Informal Procedure*, p. 142.

[3] Canon 2142.

they also admit that canonists are not agreed on this.[4] In view of the clear wording in canon 1585 and again in canon 2142 it is a little difficult to see how such an opinion could be successfully defended. All processes require a notary, and this demand is one that touches the very validity of the acts.

The oath of secrecy for the notary in such processes and the penal sanction invoked for any violation of such an oath are specifically mentioned.[5] The employment of a notary is requisite in the processes dealing with the removal of irremovable pastors,[6] the removal of removable pastors,[7] and the transfers of pastors.[8] The notary is required also in processes undertaken against clerics charged with a violation of the law of residence,[9] or with the practice of concubinage.[10] Again, a notary is necessary in the procedure against negligent pastors,[11] and in the inflicting of a suspension upon an ordinary's certified personal knowledge (*ex informata conscientia*).[12]

In the decree of the appointment of the tribunal for the ordinary process in causes of beatification and canonization the Ordinary should also appoint a notary for the process.[13]

Prior to the Code it was strictly required that the one who was appointed as notary in these processes should be chosen from among the already existing notaries.[14] Blaher notes that "all the present time the Code itself seems to insinuate as much when in canon 2013 it states '. . . notarii munere fungi potest ipsemet Curiae notarius; . . .' ."[15] In these processes, religious cannot be validly employed

[4] *Epitome Iuris Canonici,* III, n. 343.

[5] Canon 2144.

[6] Canons 2147-2156.

[7] Canons 2157-2161.

[8] Canons 2162-2167.

[9] Canons 2168-2175.

[10] Canons 2176-2181.

[11] Canons 2182-2185.

[12] Canons 2186-2194.

[13] Canon 2040, § 2.

[14] S. R. C., decr. 16 iul. 1894, *Fontes,* n. 6238.

[15] *The Ordinary Processes in Causes of Beatification and Canonization,* (The Catholic University of America Canon Law Studies, n. 268 (Washington, D. C.: The Catholic University of America Press, 1949), p. 134, footnote.

as notaries, except by way of necessity. In causes pertaining to their own religious institute they are always excluded.[16]

The printed formulas for the acts of each session of these processes are obtainable through postulators in Rome. These will be of inestimable help, of course, to the notary.[17]

---

[16] Canon 2014.

[17] There may be suggested as a general help to the notary the information afforded by Blaher's work, already cited, and by the work of Lauri-Fornari-Santarelli, *Codex pro Postulatoribus Causarum Beatificationis et Canonizationis* (4. ed., Romae: Ex Typographia Agostiniana, 1929), especially pp. 42-47.

APPENDIX

A. A suggested formula of appointment:

In nomine Domini.

Cum ex Sacrorum Canonum dispositione eligendus sit Notarius Iudicialis, Te, N. N. eligimus et deputamus in Notarium Iudicialem pro causa X (vel, ad universitatem causarum) quae apud Tribunal diocesanum agitanda est, praestitis iuramentis requisitis.

In quorum fidem, etc.

Datum............die............

N. N. Episcopus

N. N. Cancellarius

B. A suggested formula of the oath of office:

In nomine Domini.

Ego, N. N., spondeo, voveo ac iuro me rite, diligenter ac fideliter impleturum munus Notarii Iudicialis mihi commissum, posthabita quavis personarum acceptione, et secretum officii mei religiose servaturum. Sic me Deus adiuvet.

N. N. Notarius Iudicialis

CONCLUSIONS

1. A confusing use of terms has complicated the historical delineation of the judicial notary. Regardless of whatever term may have been employed in designation of his position, a notary was employed in church trials. The present writer has designated him as the judicial notary, although that term is not used in the pre-Code authors. He was a *publica persona,* but in his specific office as notary he was employed in ecclesiastical trials.

2. The office of judicial notary was known in the Roman law system. There is evidence to indicate that such a person was employed in ecclesiastical courts before the thirteenth century. The IV General Council of the Lateran (1215) established the office in a permanent and abiding manner. From the beginning this office was usually held by a cleric. For a time the office was regarded by some as unsuited for clerics. It gradually regained its good reputation and high standing.

3. It was what he did that made the judicial notary so important. He was generally competent in the notarial art before being employed by the court. His was a tedious and exacting task, with little of the prestige that attached to the higher positions in ecclesiastical tribunals. His general duties, unchanged for the most part in the pre-Code history, made him indispensable for valid judicial processes.

4. There is evidence that the notariate was regarded as one of the Minor Orders.

5. The judicial notary must be present at and attest to what transpires at every session of any judicial process.

6. Judicial acts which lack the signature of the notary are invalid; while the lack of such solemnities as the seal, although not invalidating, offers sufficient grounds for lodging an exception of suspicion regarding the authenticity of the acts in question.

7. In practice, every page of all the judicial acts forwarded to courts of appeals, including Rome, should bear the signature of the judicial notary and the seal of the court.

8. The Code affirms the control of the bishop over notaries and their appointment. The power of appointment which the bishop enjoyed by custom is now confirmed by law.

9. Experience and skill and knowledge of the law on the part of the judicial notary, while not required by law as necessary qualifications in the candidate for the office of judicial notary, will insure the securing of the formal excellence of the judicial acts, namely, a complete, faithful, and intelligent record of any process.

BIBLIOGRAPHY

SOURCES

Acta Apostolicae Sedis, Commentarium Officiale, Romae, 1909—

Acta et Decreta Concilii Plenarii Baltimorensis Tertii, A.D. MDCCCLXXXIV, Baltimore, John Murphy, 1886.

Acta et Decreta Sacrorum Conciliorum Recentiorum, Collectio Lacensis, 7 vols., Friburgi Brisgoviae: Sumptibus Herder, 1870-1892.

Acta Sanctae Sedis, 41 vols., Romae, 1865-1908.

Bouscaren, T. Lincoln, *Canon Law Digest, Supplement through 1948,* Milwaukee; Bruce Publishing Co., 1949.

Codex Iuris Canonici Pii X Pontificis Maximi iussu digestus Benedicti Papae XV auctoritate promulgatus, Romae: Typis Polyglottis Vaticanis, 1917.

Codicis Iuris Canonici Fontes, cura Emi Petri Card. Gasparri editi, 9 vols., Romae (postea Civitate Vaticana): Typis Polyglottis Vaticanis, 1923-1939. Vols. VII-IX, ed. cura et studio Emi Iustiniani Card. Seredi.

Collectanea S. Congregationis de Propaganda Fide, 2 vols., Romae: Typographia Polyglotta S.C. de Propaganda Fide, 1907.

Corpus Iuris Canonici, editio Lipsiensis secunda, post Aemilii Ludovici Richteri curas instruxit Aemilius Friedberg, 2 vols., Lipsiae, 1879-1881. Editio anastatice repetita, Lipsiae: Tauchnitz, 1928.

Corpus Iuris Civilis, Vol. I, *Institutiones,* quas recognovit Paulus Krueger; *Digesta,* quae recognovit Theodorus Mommsen, retractavit Paulus Krueger, ed. stereotypa quinta decima, Berolini: Apud Weidmannos, 1928.

———, Vol. II, *Codex Iustinianus,* quem recognovit et retractavit Paulus Krueger, ed. stereotypa decima, Berolini: Apud Weidmannos, 1929.

———, Vol. III, *Novellae,* quas recognovit Rudolfus Schoell, absolvit Guilelmus Kroll, ed. stereotypa quinta, Berolini: Apud Weidmannos, 1928.

Theodosiani Libri XVI, quos recognovit Th. Mommsen, absolvit Paulus Krueger, 2 vols., Berolini: Apud Weidmannos, 1905.

Decretales D. Gregorii Papae IX, una cum glossis restitutae, 2 vols., Romae, 1582.

Hardouin, Jean, *Acta Conciliorum et Epistolae Decretales ac Constitutiones Summorum Pontificum,* 12 vols., Parisiis, 1714-1715.

Jaffe, Philippus, *Regesta Pontificum Romanorum ab condita Ecclesia ad annum post Christum natum MCXCVIII,* 2. ed., cura G. Wattenbach, F. Kaltenbrunner (ed. annum 590); P. Ewald (anno 590-882), S. Lowenfeld (anno 882-1198), 2 vols., Lipsiae, 1885-1888.

Magnum Bullarium Romanum, 19 vols., Luxemburgi, 1727-1754.

Mansi, Ioannes, *Sacrorum Conciliorum Nova et Amplissima Collectio,* 53 vols., in 60, Paris-Leipzig-Arnhem, 1901-1927.

Pallottini, Salvator, *Collectio omnium conclusionum et resolutionum quae in causis propositis apud Sacram Congregationem Cardinalium S. Concilii Tridentini Interpretum prodierunt ab eius institutione anno MDLXIV ad annum MDCCCLX, distinctis titulis alphabetico ordine per materias digesta,* 17 vols., Romae, 1868-1893.

Potthast, Augustus, *Regesta Pontificum inde ab anno post Christum MCXCVIII ad MCCCIV,* 2 vols., Berolini, 1874-1875.

Roziere, Eugene de, *Liber Diurnus,* Paris, 1869.

Sacrae Romanae Rotae Decisiones seu Sententiae quae . . . prodierunt anno 1909—, Romae, 1912—.

Schroeder, H.J., *Canons and Decrees of the Council of Trent,* St. Louis: B. Herder, 1941.

Thesaurus Resolutionum Sacrae Congregationis Concilii, 167 vols., Romae, 1718-1908.

Thiel, A., *Epistolae Romanorum Pontificum Genuinae a S. Hilario usque ad Pelagium II,* Vol. I, *Epistolae Romanorum Pontificum a S. Hilario usque ad S. Hormisdam,* Brunsbergae, 1868.

AUTHORS

Augustine, Charles, *A Commentary on the New Code of Canon Law,* 8 vols., Vol. II, 3. ed., 1919, Vol. VII, 1921, St. Louis: B. Herder.

Baart, Peter, *Legal Formulary,* 3. ed., New York: Pustet, 1899.

Barraclough, Geoffrey, *Public Notaries and the Papal Curia,* London: Macmillan and Co., Ltd., 1934.

Benedetti, Ivo, *Ordo Iudicialis Processus Canonici Super Nullitate Matrimonii Instruendi,* 2. ed., Taurini: Marietti, 1938.

Beste, Udalricus, *Introductio in Codicem,* 2, ed., Collegeville, Minnesota: St. John's Abbey Press, 1944.

Blaher, Damian J., *The Ordinary Processes in Causes of Beatification and Canonization,* The Catholic University of America Canon Law Studies, n. 268, Washington, D.C.: The Catholic University of America Press, 1949.

Bouix, D., *Tractatus de Judiciis Ecclesiasticis,* 2 vols., Parisiis, 1855.

Canavan, Walter, *The Profession of Faith,* The Catholic University of America Canon Law Studies, n. 151, Washington, D.C.: The Catholic University of America Press, 1942.

Cappello, Felix, *Praxis Processualis,* Taurini-Romae: Marietti 1940.

Coronata, Matthaeus Conte a, *Institutiones Iuris Canonici,* 2. ed., 5 vols., Taurini: Marietti, 1939-1947.

Cerchiari, E., *Capellani Papae et Apostolicae Sedis, Auditores Causarum Sacri Palatii Apostolici seu S.R. Rotae, ab Origine ad Diem usque 20 sept. 1870,* 4 vols., Romae, 1919-1921.

Dictionnaire d'Archeologie Chretienne et de Liturgie, edited by Fernand Cabrol and Henri Leclercq, 14 vols., Paris: Librairie Letouzey et Ane, 1907-1939.

Doheny, William, *Canonical Procedure in Matrimonial Cases, I, Formal Judicial Procedure*, 2. ed., Milwaukee: Bruce Publishing Co., 1948.

———, *Canonical Procedure in Matrimonial Cases, II, Informal Procedure*, Milwaukee: Bruce Publishing Co., 1944.

———, *Practical Manual for Marriage Cases*, Milwaukee: Bruce Publishing Co., 1938.

Droste, F., and Messmer, S., *Canonical Procedure in Disciplinary and Criminal Cases of Clerics*, New York: Benziger Brothers, 1887.

Duchesne, Louis, *Le Liber Pontificalis*, 2 vols., Paris, 1886/1892.

Dugan, Henry, *The Judiciary Department of the Diocesan Curia*, The Catholic University of America Canon Law Studies, n. 26, Washington, D. C.: The Catholic University of America, 1925.

Fagnanus, Prosper, *Commentaria in Quinque Libros Decretalium*, 5 vols., Venetiis, 1696.

Ferraris, Lucius, *Prompta Bibliotheca Canonica, Iuridica, Moralis, Theologica, necnon Ascetica, Polemica, Rubricistica, Historica*, ed. noviss., 9 vols., Romae, 1885-1899.

Fournier, Edouard, *L'Origine du Vicaire General et des Autres Membres de la Curie Diocesaine*, Paris: Seminaire des Missions Etrangeres, 1940.

Fournier, Paul, *Les Officialites au Moyen Age*, Paris: Plon, 1880.

Heiner, F., *De Processu Criminali Ecclesiastico*, edidit A. Wynen, Romae: Pustet, 1912.

Hilling, Nicholas, *Procedure at the Roman Curia*, New York: Wagner, 1907.

Hincmarus, *De Ordine Palatii*, edidit Victor Krause, Hannoverae et Lipsiae, 1894.

Hostiensis, Cardinalis (Henricus de Segusia), *Commentaria in Quinque Decretalium Libros*, 5 vols., in 3, Venetiis, 1581.

———, *Summa Aurea*, Venetiis, 1570.

Lane, Loras, *Matrimonial Procedure in the Ordinary Courts of Second Instance*, The Catholic University of America Canon Law Studies, n. 253, Washington, D. C.: The Catholic University of America Press, 1947.

Ioannes Andreae, *In Quinque Decretalium Libros Novella Commentaria*, 4 vols., Venetiis, 1581.

Lauri, Aloisius — Fornari, Jos. — Santarelli, Ant., *Codex pro Postulatoribus Causarum Beatifications et Canonizationis, 4. ed., Romae* Ex Typographia Agostiniana, 1929.

Lega, M., *Praelectiones in Textum Iuris Canonici: De Iudiciis Ecclesiasticis*, 4 vols., Romae, 1896-1901.

Lega, M. — Bartoccetti, V., *Commentarius in Iudicia Ecclesiastica iuxta Codicem Iuris Canonici*, 3 vols., Romae: Anonima Libraria Cattolica Italiana, 1938-1941.

Lemieux, Delisle, *The Sentence in Ecclesiastical Procedure,* The Catholic University of America Canon Law Studies, n. 87, Washington, D.C.: The Catholic University of America, 1934.

Maroto, Philippus, *Institutiones Iuris Canonici,* 2 vols., Vol. II, Romae, 1919.

Mathias, L., *The Diocesan Curia,* Madras: The Good Pastor Press, 1947.

Metz, John E., *The Recording Judge in the Ecclesiastical Collegiate Tribunal,* The Catholic University of America Canon Law Studies, n. 287, Washington, D.C.: The Catholic University of America Press, 1949.

Migne, J.P., *Patrologiae Cursus Completus, Series Latina,* 221 vols., Parisiis, 1844-1864.

Noval, Iosephus, *Commentarium Codicis Iuris Canonici,* Liber IV, *De Processibus,* Pars I, *De Iudiciis,* Augustae Taurinorum-Romae, 1920.

Ottaviani, Alaphridus, *Compendium Iuris Publici Ecclesiastici,* Romae: Typis Polyglottis Vaticanis, 1936.

Panormitanus, Abbas (Nicholaus de Tudeschis), *Commentaria in Quinque Libros Decretalium,* 5 vols., in 7, Venetiis, 1588.

Pirhing, Ernricus, *Ius Canonicum in V Libros Decretalium,* 5 vols., Dilingae, 1674—1678.

Poole, Reginald L., *Lectures on the History of the Papal Chancery,* Cambridge: Cambridge Press, 1915.

Reiffenstuel, A., *Ius Canonicum Universum,* 7 vols., Parisiis, 1864-1870.

Roberti, Franciscus, *De Processibus,* 2 vols., Romae: Apud Aedes Facultatis Iuridicae Ad S. Apollinaris, 1926, Vol. I, 2. ed., Romae: Apud Custodiam Librariam Pontificii Instituti Utriusque Iuris, 1941.

Rota, P. *Enchiridion Confessarii et Iudicis Ecclesiastici,* Taurini: Marietti, 1884.

Prince, John E., *The Diocesan Chancellor,* The Catholic University of America Canon Law Studies, n. 167, Washington, D. C.: The Catholic University of America Press, 1942.

Savigny, Friedrich Karl von,, *Geschichte des romischen Rechts im Mittelalter,* 2. ed., 7 vols., Heidelberg, 1834-1851.

Sherman, C. P., *Roman Law in the Modern World,* 2. ed., 3 vols., New York: Baker, Voorhis & Co., 1924.

Schroeder, H. J.,*Disciplinary Decrees of the General Councils,* St. Louis: B. Herder, 1937.

Smith, S. B., *The New Procedure in Criminal and Disciplinary Causes of Ecclesiastics in the United States,* 2. ed., New York: Pustet, 1888.

Tangl, Michael, *Die papstlichen Kanzleiordnungen,* Innsbruck, 1894.

Thomassinus, Ludovicus, *Vetus et Nova Ecclesiae Disciplina circa Beneficia et Beneficiarios,* 10 vols., Magontiaci, 1787.

Vaughan, William, *Constitutions for Diocesan Courts,* The Catholic University of America Canon Law Studies, n. 210, Washington, D. C.: The Catholic University of America Press, 1944.

Vermeersch, A.—Creusen, J., *Epitome Iuris Canonici,* 3 vols., Vol. III, 6. ed., Mechliniae-Romae: H. Dessain, 1946.

Wahrmund, Ludwig, *Quellen zur Geschichte des romisch-kanonischen Processes im Mittelalter*, 5 vols., Innsbruck and Heidelberg, 1905-1931.

Wernz, F. X.—Vidal, P., *Ius Canonicum*, 7 tomes in 8 vols., Vol. II, 3. ed., a P. Aguirre recognita, 1943; Vol. VI, 1927, Romae: Apud Aedes Universitatis Gregorianae.

Willett, Robert A., *The Probative Value of Documents in Ecclesiastical Trials*, The Catholic University of America Canon Law Studies, n. 171, Washington, D. C.: The Catholic University of America Press, 1942.

Woywod, S.,—Smith, C., *A Practical Commentary on the Code of Canon Law*, revised and enlarged edition, 2 vols., New York: Joseph F. Wagner, 1948.

ARTICLES

Bastnagel, Clement V., "Testimony in Summary Cases," *The Jurist*, V (1945), 441-447.

Baumgarten, Paul M., "Die papstlichen Notare in dreizehnten, vierzehnten und funfzehnten Jahrhundert," *Gorres-Gesellschaft zur Pflege der Wissenschaft im katholischen Deutschland, Veroffentlichungen der Sektion fur Rechts und Staatswissenschaft*, IV-1 (1908), 1-68.

Brown, James C., "The Origin and Early History of the Office of Notary," *The Juridical Review*, XLVII (1935), n. 3 (pp. 201-240) and n. 4 (pp. 355-417).

Couly, August, "L'Officialite: Les Notaries ou Actuaires," *Le Canoniste*, XLVII (1925), 75-85.

Laborderie-Boulou, Pierre, "Recherches sur les Origines de la Responsabilite Notariale," *Revue Generale du Droit*, XXXVI (1912), 385-393.

Schneider, F. E., "Die romishe Rota," *Gorres-Gesellschaft zur Pflege der Wissenschaft im katholischen Deutschland, Veroffentlichungen der Sektion fur Rechts und Staatswissenschaft*, XXII (1914), 132-147.

Toso, A., "An Notarii et Advocati Munera Incompatibilia Sint in Causis Ecclesiasticis," *Jus Pontificium*, XVIII (1938), 81-84.

PERIODICALS

Analecta Iuris Pontificii, Romae, 1885-1869, Parisiis, 1872-1891.

Gorres-Gessellschaft zur Pflege der Wissenschaft im katholischen Deutschland, Veroffentlichungen der Sektion fur Rechts und Staatswissenschaft, Koln, 1908, Paderborn, 1909-1939.

Juridical Review, The, Edinburgh: Green and Son, 1888—.

Jurist, The, Washington, D. C., 1941—.

Jus Pontificium, Rome, 1921-1940.

Le Canoniste Contemporain, Paris, 1878-1922; *Le Canoniste*, Paris, 1924-1926.

Revue Generale du Droit, Paris, 1876—.

BIOGRAPHICAL NOTE

Charles Joseph Duerr was born on February 4, 1922, in Green Bay, Wisconsin. He received his elementary education at Saint Willebrord's Parochial School. After completing the high school courses at Cathedral Junior High School in Green Bay, and at Saint Norbert's High School at West DePere, Wisconsin, he entered Saint Norbert's College. The degree of Bachelor of Arts was conferred on him by Saint Norbert's College in June, 1943. He made his theological studies at the Seminary of Saint John the Baptist, Collegeville, Minnesota, and was ordained to the priesthood on June 15, 1946. He was appointed to the Diocesan Department of Education, and then to the Cathedral as a parochial assistant until September, 1947, when he entered the Graduate School of Canon Law at The Catholic University of America. From this School he received the degree of the Baccalaureate in Canon Law in June, 1948, and the degree of the Licentiate in Canon Law in June, 1949.

CANON LAW STUDIES*

1. FRERIKS, REV. CELESTINE A., C.PP.S., J.C.D., Religious Congregations in Their External Relations, 121 pp., 1916.
2. GALLIHER, REV. DANIEL M., O.P., J.C.D., Canonical Elections, 117 pp., 1917.
3. BORKOWSKI, REV. AURELIUS L., O.F.M., J.C.D., De Confraternitatibus Ecclesiasticis, 136 pp., 1918.
4. CASTILLO, REV. CAYO, J.C.D., Disertacion Historico-Canonica sobre la Potestad del Cabildo en Sede Vacante o Impedida del Vicario Capitular, 99 pp., 1919 (1918).
5. KUBELBECK, REV. WILLIAM J., S.T.B., J.C.D., The Sacred Penitentiaria and Its Relation to Faculties of Ordinaries and Priests, 129 pp., 1918.
6. PETROVITS, REV. JOSEPH J. C., S.T.D., J.C.D., The New Church Law on Matrimony, X-461 pp., 1919.
7. HICKEY, REV. JOHN J., S.T.B., J.C.D., Irregularities and Simple Impediments in the New Code of Canon Law, 100 p., 1920.
8. KLEKOTKA, REV. PETER J., S.T.B., J.C.D., Diocesan Consultors, 179 pp., 1920.
9. WANENMACHER, REV. FRANCIS, J.C.D., The Evidence in Ecclesiastical Procedure Affecting the Marriage Bond, 1920 (Printed 1935).
10. GOLDEN, REV. HENRY FRANCIS, J.C.D., Parochial Benefices in the New Code, IV-119 pp., 1921 (Printed 1925).
11. KOUDELKA REV. CHARLES J., J.C.D., Pastors, Their Rights and Duties According to the New Code of Canon Law, 211 p., 1921.
12. MELO, REV. ANTONIUS, O.F.M., J.C.D., De Exemptione Regularium, X-188 pp., 1921.
13. SCHAAF, REV. VALENTINE THEODORE, O.F.M., S.T.B., J.C.D., The Cloister, X-180 pp., 1921.
14. BURKE, REV. THOMAS JOSEPH, S.T.D., J.C.D., Competence in Ecclesiastical Tribunals, IV-117 pp., 1922.
15. LEECH, REV. GEORGE LEO, J.C.D., A Comparative Study of the Constitution "Apostolicae Sedis" and the "Codex Juris Canonici," 179 pp., 1922.
16. MOTRY, REV. HUBERT LOUIS, S.T.D., J.C.D., Diocesan Faculties According to the Code of Canon Law, II-167 pp., 1922.
17. MURPHY, REV. GEORGE LAWRENCE, J.C.D., Delinquencies and Penalties in the Administration and the Reception of the Sacraments, IV 121 pp., 1923.

* All published numbers are available from the Catholic University of America Press, 621 Michigan Ave., N. E., Washington 17, D. C., except the following numbers: 1-114 inclusive, and numbers 116, 118, 120, 122, 123, 162, and 198.

18. O'Reilly, Rev. John Anthony. S.T.B., J.C.D., Ecclesiastical Sepulture in the New Code of Canon Law, II-129 pp., 1923.
19. Michalicka, Rev. Wenceslas Cyrill, O.S.B., J.C.D., Judicial Procedure in Dismissal of Clerical Exempt Religious, 107 pp., 1923.
20. Dargin, Rev. Edward Vincent, S.T.B., J.C.D., Reserved Cases According to the Code of Canon Law, IV-103 pp, 1924.
21. Godfrey, Rev. John A., S.T.B., J.C.D., The Right of Patronage According to the Code of Canon Law, 153 pp., 1924.
22. Hagedorn, Rev. Francis Edward, J.C.D., General Legislation on Indulgences, II-154 pp., 1924.
23. King, Rev. James Ignatius, J.C.D., The Administration of the Sacraments to Dying Non-Ctholics, V-141 pp., 1924.
24. Winslow, Rev. Francis Joseph, M.M., J.C.D., Vicars and Prefects Apostolic, IV-149 pp., 1924.
25. Correa, Rev. Jose Servelion, S.T.L., J.C.D., La Potestad Legislativa de la Iglesia Catolica, IV-127 pp., 1925.
26. Dugan, Rev. Henry Francis, A.M., J.C.D., The Judiciary Department of the Diocesan Curia, 87 pp., 1925.
27. Keller, Rev. Charles Frederick, S.T.B., J.C.D., Mass Stipends, 167 pp., 1925.
28. Paschang, Rev. John Linus, J.C.D., The Sacramentals According to the Code of Canon Law, 129 pp., 1925.
29. Piontek, Rev. Cyrillus, O.F.M., S.T.B., J.C.D., De Indulto Exclaustrationis necnon Saecularizationis, XIII-289 pp., 1925.
30. Kearney, Rev. Richard Joseph, S.T.B., J.C.D., Sponsors at Baptism According to the Code of Canon Law, IV-127 pp., 1925.
31. Bartlet, Rev. Chester Joseph, A.M., *LL.B.*, J.C.D., The Tenure of Parochial Property in the United States of America, V-108 pp., 1926.
32. Kilker, Rev. Adrian Jerome, J.C.D., Extreme Unction, V-425 pp., 1926.
33. McCormick, Rev. Robert Emmett, J.C.D., Confessors of Religious, VIII-266 pp., 1926.
34. Miller, Rev. Newton Thomas, J.C.D., Founded Masses According to the Code of Canon Law, VII-93 pp., 1926.
35. Roelker, Rev. Edward G., S.T.D., J.C.D., Principles of Privilege According to the Code of Canon Law, XI-166 pp., 1926.
36. Bakalarczyk, Rev. Richardus, M.I.C., J.U.D., De Novitiatu, VIII-203 pp., 1927.
37. Pizzuti, Rev. Lawrence, O.F.M., J.Z.L., De Parochis Religiouis, 1927. (Not Printed.)
38. Bliley, Rev. Nicholas Martin, O.S.B., J.C.D., Altars According to the Code of Canon Law, XIX-132 pp., 1927.
39. Brown, Mr. Brendan Francis, A.B., LL.M., J.U.D., The Canonical Juristic Personality with Special Reference to its Status in the United States of America, V-212 pp., 1927.

40. CAVANAUGH, REV. WILLIAM THOMAS, C.P., J.U.D., The Reservation of the Blessed Sacrament, VIII-101 pp., 1927.
41. DOHENY, REV. WILLIAM J., C.S.C., A.B., J.U.D., Church Property: Models of Acquisition, X-118 pp., 1927.
42. FELDHAUS, REV. ALOYSIUS H., C.PP.S., J.C.D., Oratories, IX-141 pp., 1927.
43. KELLY, REV. JAMES PATRICK, A.B., J.C.D., The Jurisdiction of the Simple Confessor, X-208 pp., 1927.
44. NEUBERGER, REV. NICHOLAS J., J.C.D., Canon 6 or the Relation of the Codex Juris Canonici to the Preceding Legislation, V-95 pp.. 1927.
45. O'KEEFE, REV. GERALD MICHAEL, J.C.D., Martimonial Dispensations, Powers of Bishops, Priests, and Confessors, VIII-232 pp., 1927.
46. QUIGLEY, REV. JOSEPH, *A.M.*, A.B., J.C.D., Condemned Societies, 139 pp., 1927.
47. ZAPLOTNIK, REV. JOHANNES LEO. J.C.D., De Vicariis Foraneis, X-142 pp., 1927.
48. DUSKIE, REV. JOHN ALOYSIUS, A.B., J.C.D., The Canonical Status of the Orientals in the United States, VIII-196 pp., 1928.
49. HYLAND, REV. JOSEPH EDWARD, J.C.D., Excummunications, Its Nature, Historical Development and Effects, VII-181 pp., 1928.
50. REINMANN, REV. GERALD JOSEPH, O.M.C., J.C.D., The Third Order Secular of Saint Francis, 201 pp., 1928.
51. SCHENK, REV. FRANCIS J., J.C.D., The Matrimonial Impediments of Mixed Religion and Disparity of Cult, XVI-318 pp., 1929.
52. COADY, REV. JOHN JOSEPH, S.T.D., J.U.D., A.M., The Appointment of Pastors, VIII-150 pp., 1929.
53. KAY, REV. THOMAS HENRY, J.C.D., Competence in Matrimonial Procedure, VIII-164 pp., 1929.
54. TURNER, REV. SIDNEY JOSEPH, C.P., J.U.D., The Vow of Poverty, XLIX-217 pp., 1929.
55. KEARNEY, REV. RAYMOND A., A.B., S.T.D., J.C.D., The Principles of Delegation, VII-149 pp., 1929.
56. CONRAN, REV. EDWARD JAMES, A.B., J.C.D., The Interdict, V-163 pp. 1930.
57. O'NEIL, REV. WILLIAM H., J.C.D., Papal Rescripts of Favor, VII-218 pp., 1930.
58. BASTNAGEL, REV. CLEMENT VINCENT, J.U.D., The Appointment of Parochial Adjutants and Assisants, VX-257 pp., 1930.
59. FERRY, REV. WILLIAM A., A.B., J.C.D., Stole Fees, V-136 pp., 1930.
60. COSTELLO, REV. JOHN MICHAEL, A.B., J.C.D., Domicile and Quasi-Domicile, VII-201 pp., 1930.
61. KREMER, REV. MICHAEL NICHOLAS, A.B., S.T.B., J.C.D., Church Support in the United States, VI-136 pp., 1930.
62. ANGULO, REV. LUIS, C.M., J.C.D., Legislation de la Iglesia sobre la intencion en la application de la Santa Misa, VII-104 pp. 1931.

63. Frey, Rev. Wolfgang Norbert, O.S.B., A.B., J.C.D., The Act of Religious Profession, VII-174 pp., 1931.
64. Roberts, Rev. James Brendan, A.B., J.C.D., The Banns of Marriage, XIV-140 pp., 1931.
65. Ryder, Rev. Raymond Aloysius, A.B., J.C.D., Simony, IX-151 pp., 1931.
66. Campagna, Rev. Angelo, Ph.D., J.U.D., Il Vicario Generale del Vescovo, VII-205 pp., 1931.
67. Cox, Rev. Joseph Godfrey, A.B., J.C.D., The Administration of Seminaries, VI-124 pp., 1931.
68. Gregory, Rev. Donald J., J.U.D., The Pauline Privilege, XV-165 pp., 1931.
69. Donohue, Rev. John F., J.C.D., The Impediment of Crime, VII-110 pp., 1931.
70:. Dooley, Rev. Eugene A., O.M.I., J.C.D., Church Law on Sacred Relics, IX-143 pp., 1931.
71. Orth, Rev. Clement Raymond, O.M.C., J.C.D., The Approbation of Religious Institutes, 171 pp., 1931.
72. Pernicone, Rev. Joseph M., A.B., J.C.D., The Ecclesiastical Prohibition of Books, XII-267 pp., 1932.
73. Clinton, Rev. Connell, A.B., J.C.D., The Paschal Precept, IX-108 pp., 1932.
74. Donnelly, Rev. Francis B., A.M., S.T.L., J.C.D., The Diocesan Synod, VIII-125 pp., 1932.
75. Torrente, Rev. Camilo, C.M.F., J.C.D., Las Procesiones Sagradas, V-145 pp., 1932.
76. Murphy, Rev. Edwin J., C.PP.S., J.C.D., Suspension Ex Informata Conscientia, XI-122 pp., 1932.
77. MacKenzie, Rev. Eric F., A.M., S.T.L., J.C.D., The Delict of Hersey in its Commission, Penalization, Absolution, VII-124 pp., 1932.
78. Lyons, Rev. Avitus E., S.T.B., J.C.D., The Colegiate Tribunal of First Instance, XI-147 pp., 1932.
79. Connolly, Rev. Thomas A., J.C.D., Appeals, XI-195 pp., 1932.
80. Sangmeister, Rev. Joseph V., A.B., J.C.D., Force and Fear as Precluding Matrimonial Consent, V-211 pp., 1932.
81. Jaeger, Rev. Leo A., A.B., J.C.D., The Administration of Vacant and Quasi-Vacant Episcopal Sees in the United States, IX-229 pp., 1932.
82. Rimlinger, Rev. Herbert T., J.C.D., Error Invalidating Matrimonial Consent, VII-79 pp., 1932.
83. Barrett, Rev. John D. M., S.S., J.C.D., A Comparative Study of the Third Plenary Council of Baltimore and the Code, IX-221 pp., 1932.
84. Carberry, Rev. John J., Ph.D., S.T.D., J.C.D., The Puridical Form of Marriage, X-177 pp., 1934. œ
85. Dolan, Rev. John L., A.B., J.C.D., The Defensor Vinculi, XII-157 pp., 1934.

86. Hannan, Rev. Jerome D., A.M., S.T.D., LL.B., J.C.D., The Canon Law of Wills, IX-517 pp., 1934.
87. Lemieux, Rev. Delise A., A.M., J.C.D., The Sentence in Ecclesiastical Procedure, IX-131 pp., 1934.
88. O'Rourke, Rev. James J., A.B., J.C.D., Parish Registers, VII-109 pp., 1934.
89. Timlin, Rev. Bartholomew, O.F.M., A.M., J.C.D., C.onditional Matrimonial Consent, X-381 pp., 1934.
90. Wahl, Rev. Francis X., A.B., J.C.D., The Matrimonial Impediments of Consanguinity and Affinity, VI-125 pp., 1934.
91. White, Rev. Robert J., A.B., LL.B., S.T.B., J.C.D., Canonical Ante-Nuptial Promises and the Civil Law, VI-152 pp., 1934.
92. Herrera, Rev. Antonio Parra, O.C.D., J.C.D., Legislation Ecclesiastica sobra el Ayuno y la Abstinencia, XI-191 pp., 1935.
93. Kennedy, Rev. Edwin J., J.C.D., The Special Matrimonial Process in Cases of Evident Nullity, X-165 pp., 1935.
94. Manning, Rev. John J., A.B., J.C.D., Presumption of Law in Matri-Monial Procedure, XI-111 pp., 1935.
95. Moeder, Rev. John M., J.C.D., The Proper Bishop for Ordination and Dimissorial Letters, VII-135 pp., 1935.
96. O'Mara, Rev. William A., A.B., J.C.D., Canonical Causes for Matrimonial Dispensations, IX-155 pp., 1935.
97. Reilly, Rev. Peter, J.C.D., Residence of Pastors, IX-81 pp., 1935.
98. Smith, Rev. Mariner T., O.P., S.T.Lr., J.C.D., The Penal Law for Religious, VII-169 pp., 1935.
99. Whalen, Rev. Donald W., A.M.. J.C.D., The Value of Testimonial Evidence in Matrimonial Procedure, XIII-297 pp., 1935.
100. Cleary, Rev. Joseph F., J.C.D., Canonical Limitations on the Alienation of Church Property, VIII-141 pp., 1936.
101. Glynn, Rev. John C., J.C.D., The Promoter of Justice, XX-337 pp., 1936.
102. Brennan, Rev. James H., SS., M.A., S.T.B., J.C.D., The Simple Convalidation of Marriage, VI-135 pp., 1937.
103. Brunini, Rev. Joseph Bernard, J.C.D., The Clerical Obligations of Canons 139 and 142, X-121 pp., 1937.
104. Connor, Rev. Maurice, A.B., J.C.D., The Administrative Removal of Pastors, VIII-159 pp., 1937.
105. Guilfoyle, Rev. Merlin Joseph, J.C.D., Custom, XI-144 pp., 1937.
106. Hughes, Rev. James Austin, A.B., A.M., J.C.D., Witnesses in Criminal Trials of Clerics, IX-140 pp., 1937.
107. Jansen, Rev. Raymond J., A.B., S.T.L., J.C.D., Canonical Provisions for Catechetical Instruction, VII-153 pp., 1937.
108. Kealy, Rev. John James, A.B., J.C.D., The Introductory Libellus in Church Court Procedure, XI-121 pp., 1937.

109. McManus, Rev. James Edward, C.SS.R., J.C.D., The Administration of Temporal Goods in Religious Institutes, XVI-196 pp., 1937.
110. Moriarty, Rev. Eugene James, J.C.D., Oaths in Ecclesiastical Courts, X-115 pp., 1937.
111. Rainer, Rev. Elicius George, C.SS.R., J.C.D., Suspension of Clerics, XVII-249 pp., 1937.
112. Reilly, Rev. Thomas F., C.SS.R., J.C.D., Visitation of Religious, VI-195 pp., 1938.
113. Moriarity, Rev. Francis E., C.SS.R., J.C.D., The Extraordinary Absolution from Censures, XV-334 pp., 1938.
114. Connolly, Rev. Nicholas P., J.C.D., The Canonical Erection of Parishes, X-132 pp., 1938.
115. Donovan, Rev. James Joseph, J.C.D., The Pastor's Obligation in Prenuptial Investigation, XII-322 pp., 1938.
116. Harrigan, Rev. Robecrt J., M.A., S.T.B., J.C.D., The Radical Sanation of Invalid Marrages, VIII-208 pp., 1938.
117. Boffa, Rev. Conrad Humbert, J.C.D., Canonical Provisions for Catholic Schools, VII-211 pp., 1939.
118. Parsons, Rev. Anscar John, O.M.Cap., J.C.D., Canonical Elections, XII-236 pp., 1939.
119. Reilly, Rev. Edward Michael, A.B., J.C.D., The General Norms of Dispensation, XII-156 pp., 1939.
120. Ryan, Rev. Gerald Aloysius, A.B., J.C.D., Principles of Episcopal Jurisdiction, XII-173 pp., 1939.
121. Burton, Rev. Francis James, C.S.C., A.B., J.C.D., A Commentary on Canon 1125, X-222 pp., 1940.
122. Miaskiewicz, Rev. Francis Sigismund, J.C.D., Supplied Jurisdiction According to Canon 209, XII-340 pp., 1940.
123. Rice, Rev. Patrick William, A.B., J.C.D., Proof of Death in Prenuptial Investigation, VIII-156 pp., 1940.
124. Anglin, Rev. Thomas Francis, M.S., J.C.D., The Eucharistic Fast, VIII-183 pp., 1941.
125. Coleman, Rev. John Jerome, J.C.D., The Minister of Confirmation, VI-153 pp., 1941.
126. Downs, Rev. John Emmanuel, A.B., J.C.D., The Concept of Clerical Immunity, XI-163 pp., 1941.
127. Esswein, Rev. Anthony Albert, J.C.D., Extrajudicial Penal Powers of Ecclesiastical Superiors, X-144 pp., 1941.
128. Farrell, Rev. Benjamin Francis, M.A., S.T.L., J.C.D., The Rights and Duties of the Local Ordinary Regarding Congregations of Women Religious of Pontifical Approval, V-195 pp., 1941.
129. Feeney, Rev. Thomas John, A.B., S.T.L., J.C.D., Restitutio in Integrum, VI-169 pp., 1941.

130. FINDLAY, REV. STEPHEN WILLIAM, O.S.B., A.B., J.C.D., Canonical Norms Governing the Deposition and Degradation of Clerics, XVII-279 pp., 1941.
131. GOODWINE, REV. JOHN, A.B., S.T.L., J.C.D., The Right of the Church to Acquire Property, VIII-119 pp., 1941.
132. HESTON, REV. EDWARD LOUIS, C.S.D.. Ph.D., S.T.D., J.C.D., The Alienation of Church Property in the United States, XII-222 pp., 1941.
133. HOGAN, REV. JAMES JOHN, A.B., S.T.L., J.C.D., Judicial Advocates and Procurators, XIII-200 pp., 1941.
134. KEALY, REV. THOMAS M., A.B., Litt.B., J.C.D., Dowry of Women Religious, IX-152 pp., 1941.
135. KEENE, REV. MICHAEL JAMES, O.S.B., J.C.D., Religious Ordinaries and Canon 198, V-164 pp., 1942.
136. KERLIN, REV. CHARLES A., S.S., M.A., S.T.B., J.C.D., The Privation of Christian Burial, XVI-279 pp., 1941.
137. LOUIS, REV. WILLIAM FRANCIS, M.A., J.C.D., Diocesan Archives, X-101 pp., 1941.
138. McDEVITT, REV. GILBERT JOSEPH, A.B., J.C.D., Legitimacy and Legitimation, X-247 pp., 1941.
139. McDONOUGH, REV. THOMAS JOSEPH, A.B., J.C.D., Apostolic Administrators. X-217 pp., 1941.
140. MEIER, REV. CARL ANTHONY, A.B., J.C.D., Penal Administrative Procedure Against Negligent Pastors, XI-240 pp., 1941.
141. SCHMIDT, REV. JOHN ROGG, A.B., J.C.D., The Principles of Authentic Interpretation in Canon 17 of the Code of Canon Law, XII-331 pp., 1941.
142. SLAFKOSKY, REV. ANDREW LEONARD, A.B., J.C.D., The Canonical Episcopal Visitation of the Diocese, X-197 pp, .1941.
143. SWOBODA, REV. INNOCENT ROBERT, O.F.M., J.C.D., Ignorance in Relation to the Imputability of Delicts, IX-271 pp., 1941.
144. DUBE, REV. ARTHUR JOSEPK, A.B., J.C.D., The General Principles for the Reckoning of Time in Canon Law, VIII-299 pp., 1941.
145. McBRIDE, REV. JAMES T., A.B., J.C.D., Incardinaton and Excardination of Seculars, XX-585 pp., 1941.
146. KROL, REV. JOHN T., J.C.D., The Defendant in Ecclesiastical Trials, XII-207 pp., 1942.
147. COMYNS, REV. JOSEPH J., C.SS.R., A.B., J.C.D., Papal and Episcopal Administration of Church Property, XIV-155 pp., 1942.
148. BARRY, REV. GARRETT FRANCIS, O.M.I., J.C.D., Violation of the Cloister, XII-260 pp., 1942.
149. BOLDUC, REV. GATIEN, C.S.V., A.B., S.T.L., J.C.D., Les Etudes dans les Religions Clericales, VIII-155 pp., 1942
150. BOYLE, REV. DAVID JOHN, M.A., J.C.D., The Juridic Effeccts of Moral Certitude on Pre-Nuptial Guarantees, XII-188 pp., 1942.

151. Canavan, Rev. Walter Joseph, M.A., Litt.D., J.C.D., The Profession of Faith, XII-143 pp., 1942.
152. Desrochers, Rev. Bruno, A.B., Ph.L., S.T.B., J.C.D., Le Premier Concile Plenier de Quebec et le Code de Droit Canonique, XIV-186 pp., 1942.
153. Dillon, Rev. Robert Edward, A.B., J.C.D., Common Law Marriage, X-148 pp., 1942.
154. Dodwell, Rev. Edward John, Ph.D., S.T.B., J.C.D., The Time and Place for the Celebration of Marriage, X-156 pp., 1942.
155. Donnellan, Rev. Thomas Andrew, A.B., J.C.D., The Obligation of the Missa pro Populo, VII-131 pp., 1942.
156. Eltz, Rev. Louis Anthony, A.B., J.C.D., Cooperation in Crime, XII-208 pp., 1942.
157. Gass, Rev. Sylvester Francis, M.A., J.C.D., Ecclesiastical Pensions, XI-206 pp., 1942.
158. Guiniven, Rev. John Joseph, C.SS.R., J.C.D., The Precept of Hearing Mass, XIV-188 pp., 1942.
159. Gluczynski, Rev. John Theophilus, J.C.D., The Desecration and Violation of Churches, X-126 pp., 1942.
160. Hammill, Rev. John Leo, M.A., J.C.D., The Obligations of the Traveler According to Canon 14, VIII-204 pp., 1942.
161. Haydt, Rev. John Joseph, A.B., J.C.D., Reserved Benefices, XI-148 pp., 1942.
162. Huser, Rev. Roger John, O.F.M., A.B., J.C.D., The Crime of Abortion in Canon Law, XII-187 pp., 1942.
163. Kearney, Rev. Francis Patrick, A.B., S.T.L., J.C.D., The Principles of Canon 1127, X-162 pp., 1942.
164. Linahen, Rev. Leo James, S.T.L., J.C.D., De Absolutione Complicis In Peccato Turpi, 114 pp., 1942.
165. McCloske, Rev. Joseph Aloysius, A.B., J.C.D., The Subject of Ecclesiastical Law According to Canon 12, XVII-246 pp., 1942.
166. O,Neill, Rev. Francis Joseph, C.SS.R., J.C.D., The Dismissal of Religious in Temporary Vows, XIII-220 pp., 1942.
167. Prince, Rev. John Edward, A.B., S.T.B., J.C.D., The Diocesan Chancellor, X-136 pp., 1942.
168. Rieser, Rev. Albert Joseph, C.SS.R., J.C.D., Apostates and Fugitives from Religious Institutes, IX-168 pp., 1942.
169. Stenger, Rev. Joseph Bernard, J.C.D., The Mortgaging of Church Property, 186 pp., 1942.
170. Waldron, Rev. Joseph Francis, A.B., J.C.D., The Minister of Baptism, XII-197 pp., 1942.
171. Willett, Rev. Robert Albert, J.C.D., The Probative Value of Documents in Ecclesiastical Trials, X-124 pp., 1942.
172. Woeber, Rev. Edward Martin, M.A., J.C.D., The Interpellations, XII-161 pp., 1942.

173. Benko, Rev. Matthew Aloysius, O.S.B., M.A., J.C.D., The Abbot *Nullius*, XVI-148 pp., 1943.

174. Christ, Rev. Joseph James, M.A., S.T.L., J.C.D., Dispensation from Vindicative Penalties, XIV-285 pp., 1943.

175. Clancy, Rev. Patrick M. J., O.P., A.B., S.T.L., J.C.D., The Local Religious Superior, X-229 pp, 1943

176. Clarke, Rev. Thomas James, J.C.D., Parish Societies, XII-147 pp., 1943.

177. Connolly, Rev. John Patrick, S.T.L., J.C.D., Synodal Examiners and Parish Priest Consultors, X-223 pp., 1943.

178. Drumm, Rev. William Martin, A.B., J.C.D., Hospital Chaplains, XII-175 pp., 1943.

179. Flanagan, Rev. Bernard Joseph, A.B., S.T.L., J.C.D., The Canonical Erection of Religious Houses, X-147 pp., 1943.

180. Kelleher, Rev. Stephen Joseph, A.B., S.T.B., J.C.D., Discussions with Non-Catholics: Canonical Legislation, X-93 pp., 1943.

181. Lewis, Rev. Gordian, C.P., J.C.D., Chapters in Religious Institutes, XII-169 pp., 1943.

182. Mark, Rev. Adolph, J.C.D., The Declaration of Nullity of Marriages Contracted Outside the Church, X-151 pp., 1943.

183. Matulenas, Rev. Raymond Anthony, O.S.B., A.B., J.C.D., Communication, a Source of Privileges, XII-225 pp., 1943.

184. O'Leary, Rev. Charles Gerald, C.SS.R., J.C.D., Religious Dismissed After Perpetual Profession, X-213 pp., 1943.

185. Power, Rev. Cornelius Micheal, J.C.D., The Blessing of Cemeteries, XII-231 pp., 1943.

186. Shuhler, Rev. Ralph Vincent, O.S.A., J.C.D., Privileges of Regulars to Absolve and Dispense, XII-195 pp., 1943.

187. Ziolkowski, Rev. Thaddeus Stanislaus, A.B., J.C.D., The Consecration and Blessing of Churches, XII-151 pp., 1943.

188. Heneghan, Rev. John Joseph, S.T.D., J.C.D., The Marriages of Unworthy Catholics: Canons 1065 and 1066, XVI-213 pp., -944.

189. Carroll, Rev. Coleman Francis, M.A., S.T.L., J.C.L., Charitable Institutions.

190. Ciesluk, Rev. Joseph Edward, Ph.B., S.T.L., J.C.D., National Parishes in the United States, VI-178 pp., 1944.

191. Coburn, Rev. Vincent Paul, A.B., J.C.D., Marriages of Conscience, XII-172 pp., 1944.

192. Conners, Rev. Charles Paul, C.S.Sp., A.B., J.C.D., Extra-Judicial Procurators in the Code of Canon Law, X-94 pp., 1944.

193. Coyle, Rev. Paul Raymond, A.B., J.C.D., Judicial Exceptions, X-142 pp., 1944.

194. Fair, Rev. Bartholomew Francis, A.B., S.T.L., J.C.D., The Impediment of Abduction, XII-122 pp., 1944.

195. Gallagher, Rev. Thomas Raphael, O.P., A.B., S.T.Lr., J.C.D., The Examination of the Qualities of the Ordinand, X-166 pp., 1944.
196. Gannon, Rev. John Mark, S.T.L., J.C.D., The Interstices Required for the Promotion to Orders, XII-100 pp., 1944.
197. Goldsmith, Rev. J. William, B.C.S., S.T.L., J.C.D., The Competence of Church and State over Marriage—Disputed Points, X-128 pp., 1944.
198. Goodwine, Rev. Joseph Gerald, A.B., S.T.D., J.C.D., The Reception of Converts, XIV-326 pp., 1944.
199. Kowalski, Rev. Romuald Eugene, O.F.M., A.B., J.C.D., Sustenance of Religious Houses of Regulars, X-174 pp., 1944.
200. McCoy, Rev. Alan Edward, O.F.M., J.C.D., Force and Fear in Relation to Delictual Imputability and Penal Responsibility, XII-160 pp., 1944.
201. McDevitt, Rev. Vincent John, Ph.B., S.T.L., J.C.L., Perjury
202. Martin, Rev. Thomas Owen, Ph.D., S.T.D., J.C.D., Adverse Possession, Prescription and Limitation of Actions: The Canonical "Praescriptio," XX-208 pp., 1944.
203. Miklosovic, Rev. Paul John, A.B., J.C.L., Attempted Marriages and Their Consequent Juridic Effects.
204. Mundy, Rev. Thomas Maurice, A.B., S.T.L., J.C.D.. The Union of Parishes, X—164 pp., 1944.
205. O'Dea, Rev. John Coyle, A.B., J.C.D., The Matrimonial Impediment of Nonage, VIII-126 pp., 1944.
206. Olalia, Rev. Alexander Ayson, S.T.L., J.C.D., A Comparative Study of the Christian Constitution of States and the Constitution of the Philippine Commonwealth, XII—136 pp., 1944.
207. Poisson, Rev. Pierre-Marie, C.S.C., A.B., Ph.L., Th.L., J.C.L., Droits Patrimoniaux des Maisons et des Eglises Religieuses.
208. Stadalnikas, Rev. Casimir Joseph, M.I.C., J.C.D., Reservation of Censures, X-141 pp., 1944.
209 Shllivan, Rev. Eugene Henry, S.T.L., J.C.D., Proof of the Reception of the Sacraments, X—165 pp., 1944.
210. Vaughan, Rev. William Edward, J.C.D., Constitutions for Diocesan Courts, X-210 pp., 1944.
211. Pqro, Rev. Gino, S.T.D., J.C.L., The Right of Apoltolic Legation.
212. Balzer, Rev. Ralph Francis, C.P., J.C.D., The Computation of Time in a Canonical Novitiate, X—227 pp., 1945.
213. Dougherty, Rev. John Whelan, A.B., S.T.L., J.C.D., De Inquisitione Speciali, XII—95 pp., 1945.
214. Dziob, Rev. Micheal Walter, J.C.D., The Sacred Congregation for the Oriental Church, XII—181 pp., 1945.
215. Eidenschink, Rev. John Albert, *O.S.B., B.A., J.C.D.*, The Election of Bishops in the Letters of Pope Gregory the Great, VII—200 pp., 1945.

216. GILL, REV. NICHOLAS, C.P., J.C.D., The Spiritual Prefect in Clerical Religious Houses of Study, X—140 pp., 1945.
217. HYNES, REV. HARRY GERARD, S.T.L., J.C.D., The Privileges of Cardinals, XII-183 pp., 1945.
218. MCDEVITT, REV. GERALD VINCENT, S.T.L., J.C.D., The Renunciation of an Ecclesiastical Office, XIV—179 pp., 1945.
219. MANNING, REV. JOSEPH LEROY, J.C.D., The Free Conferral of Offices, VIII—116 pp., 1945.
220. MEYER, REV. LOUIS G., O.S.B., A.B., S.T.B., J.C.D., Alms-Gathering by Religious, XII-163 pp., 1945.
221. O'DONNELL, REV. CLETUS FRANCIS, M.A., J.C.D., The Marriage of Minors, XII-268 pp., 1945.
222. PRUNSKIS, REV. JOSEPH, J.C.D., Comparative Law, Ecclesiastical and Civil, in Lithuanian Concordat, X-161 pp., 1945.
223. SWEENEY, REV. FRANCIS PATRICK, C.SS.R., J.C.D., The Reduction of Clerics to the Lay State, X-199 pp., 1945.
224. VOGELPOHL, REV. HENRY JOHN, J.C.D., The Simple Impediments to Holy Orders, XVI-190 pp., 1945.
225. BROCKHAUS, REV. THOMAS AQUINAS, O.S.B., A.B., J.C.D., Religious who Are Known as *Conversi*, X-127 pp., 1945.
226. GRIESE, REV. N. ORVILLE, S.T.D., J.C.D., The Marriage Contract and the Procreation of Offspring, XVI-224 pp., 1946.
227. BOUDREAUX, REV. WARREN LOUIS, J.C.D., The "*ab acatholicis nati*" of Canon 1099, § 2, XII-110 pp., 1946.
228. BOWE, REV. THOMAS JOSEPH, A.B., J.C.D., Religious Superioresses, VIII-206 pp., 1946.
229. DIEDERICHS, REV. MICHAEL FERDINAND, S.C.J., J.C.D., The Jurisdiction of the Latin Ordinaries over their Oriental Subjects, XIV-153 pp., 1946.
230. DINGMAN, REV. MAURICE JOHN, A.B., S.T.L., J.C.L., The Plaintiff in Contentious Trials.
231. FRISON, REV. BASIL, C.M.F., M.MUS., J.C.D., The Retroactivity of Law, X1221 pp., 1946.
232. GALVIN, REV. WILLIAM ANTHONY, M.A., J.C.D., The Administrative Transfer of Pastors, XII-288 pp., 1946.
233. GORACY, REV. JOSEPH C., J.C.L., The Diriment Matrimonial Impediment of Major Orders.
234. HALE, REV. JOSEPH FRANCIS, M.A., S.T.L., J.C.L., The Pastor of Burial.
235. HENRY, REV. JOSEPH ARTHUR, A.B., J.C.D., The Mass and Holy Communion: Inter-Ritual Law, XII-138 pp., 1946.
236. LINENBERGER, REV. HERBERT, C.PP.S., J.C.L., The False Denunciation of an Innocent Confessor.
237. LOWRY, REV. JAMES MARTIN, A.B., J.C.D., Dispensation from Private Vows, XII-266 pp., 1946.

238. LYNCH, REV. GEORGE EDWARD, A.B., S.T.L., J.C.D., Coadjutors and Auxiliaries of Bishops, X-107 pp., 1947.

239. LYNCH, REV. TIMOTHY, M.S.SS.T., J.C.D., Contracts between Bishops and Religious Congregations, XIV-232 pp., 1946.

240. MCCLUNN, REV. JUSTIN DAVID, A.B., S.T.L., J.C.D., Administrative Recourse, VII-142 pp., 1946.

241. LOHMULLER, REV. MARTIN NICHOLAS, A.B., J.C.D., The Promulgation of Law., XII-140 pp., 1947.

242. MCGRATH, REV. JAMES, A.B., J.C.D., The Privilege of the Canon, XII-156 pp., 1946.

243. MARBACH, REV. JOSEPH FRANCIS, A.B., J.C.D., Marriage Legislation for the Catholics of the Oriental Rites in the United States and Canada, XIV-314 pp., 1946.

244. SHIMKUS, REV. BERNARD ALOYSIUS, A.B., J.C.L., The Determination and Transfer of Rite.

245. SMITH, REV. VINCENT MICHAEL, A.B., S.T.L., J.C.L., Ignorance Affecting Matrimonial Consent.

246. WACHTRLE, REV. PAUL ANTHONY, A.B., J.C.L., The Baptism of the Children of Non-Catholics.

247. CROTTY, REV. MATTHEW MICHAEL, J.C.D., The Recipient of First Holy Communion, X-142 pp., 1947.

248. EAGLETON, REV. GEORGE, J.C.L., The Quinuqennial Faculties, Formula IV.

249. GIBBONS, REV. MARION LEO, C.M., J.C.D., Domicile of the Wife Unlawfully Separated from Her Husband, XIV-171 pp., 1947.

250. KELLY, REV. BERNARD MATTHEW, S.T.L., J.C.D., The Functions Reserved to Pastors, X-150 pp., 1947.

251. KILCULLEN, REV. THOMAS JOHN, LL.M., J.C.D., The Collegiate Moral Persons as Party Litigant, X-150 pp., 1947.

252. LAFONTAINE, REV. GERMAIN JOSEPH, W.F., J.C.L., Relations Canoniques entre le Missionaire et Ses Superieurs.

253. LANE, REV. LORAS THOMAS, J.C.L., Matrimonial Procedure in Ordinary Court of Second Instance.

255. MCNICHOLAS, REV. TIMOTHY JOSEPH, J.C.D., The *Septimae Manus* Witness, XII-133 pp., 1947 (printed 1949).

268. BLAHER, REV. DAMIAN JOSEPH, O.F.M., A.B., J.C.D., The Ordinary Processes in Causes of Beatification and Canonization, XVI-290 pp., 1948 (printed 1949).

269. CLUNE, REV. ROBERT BELL, B.A., J.C.D., The Judicial Interrogation of the Parties, XII-142 pp., 1948.

270. COURTEMANCHE, REV. BASIL F., B.A., J.C.D., The Total Simulation of Matrimonial Consent, XX-120 pp., 1948.

273. FREKING, REV. FREDERICK W., A.B., S.T.B., J.C.D., The Canonical Installation of Pastors, XII-210 pp., 1948.

274. Fulton, Rev. Thomas B., J.C.D., Prenuptial Investigation, XII-190 pp., 1948.

275. Godley, Rev. James P., J.C.D., Time and Place for the Celebration of Mass, X-206 pp., 1948 (printed 1949).

276. Kane, Rev. Thomas A., A.B., B.S., J.C.D., The Jurisdiction of the Patriarchs of the Major Sees in Antiquity and in the Middle Ages, XII-153 pp., 1948 (printed 1949).

277. Kennedy, Rev. Andrew A., J.C.L., The Annual Pastoral Report to the Local Ordinary.

278. Konrad, Rev. Joseph George, J.C.D., Transfer of Religious to Another Community, VIII-284 pp., 1948 (printed 1949).

280. McCartney, Rev. Marcellus Anthony, O.F.M., M.A., J.C.D., Faculties of Regular Confessors, XII-164 pp., 1948 (printed 1949).

288. Reinhardt, Rev. Marion J., S.T.L., J.C.D., The Rogatory Commission, XIII-182 pp., 1949.

291. Allgeier, Rev. Joseph L., J.C.D., The Canonical Obligation of Preaching in Parish Churches, X-115 pp., 1949 (printed 1950).

292. Cahill, Rev. Daniel R., J.C.D., The Custody of the Holy Eucharist, XVI-178 pp., 1949 (printed 1950).

294. Knopke, Rev. Roch F., O.F.M., J.C.D., Reverential Fear in Matrimonial Cases in Asiatic Countries: Rota Cases, XII-112 pp., 1949.

295. Lavelle, Rev. Howard D., J.C.D., The Obligation of Holding Sacred Missions in Parishes, XVI-142 pp., 1949.

297. Noone, Rev. John J., J.C.D., Nullity in Judicial Acts, X-147 pp., 1949 (printed 1950).

300. Cook, Rev. John P., J.C.D., Ecclesiastical Communities and Their Ability to Induce Legal Customs, XII-152 pp., 1949 (printed 1950).

301. Fazzalaro, Rev. Francis J., J.C.D., The Place for the Hearing of Confessions, X-150 pp., 1949 (printed 1950).

302. Hannan, Rev. Philip M., J.C.D., The Canonical Concept of *Congrua Sustentatio* for the Secular Clergy, XII-237 pp., 1949 (printed 1950).

303. Quinn, Rev. Hugh G., S.T.L., J.C.L., The Particular Penal Precept.

304. Gallagher, Rev. John F., J.C.L., The Matrimonial Impediment of Public Propriety.

305. Welsh, Rev. Thomas J., J.C.L., The Use of the Portable Altar.

306. Waters, Rev. Joseph L., S.S.J., J.C.L., The Probation in Societies of Quasi-Religious.

307. Regan, Rev. Michael J., J.C.L., Canon 16.

308. Byrne, Rev. Harry J., J.C.L., Investment of Church Funds.

309. Gallagher, Rev. Thomas V., J.C.L., The Rejection of Judicial Witnesses and Testimony.

310. Chatham, Rev. Josiah G., Ph.B., S.T.L., J.C.L., Force and Fear as Invalidating Marriage: The Element of Injustice.

311. Brown, Rev. James Victor, O.R.S.A., J.C.L., The Invalidating Effects of Force, Fear, and Fraud upon the Canonical Novitiate.

312. DUERR, REV. CHARLES J., B.A., J.C.L., The Judicial Notary.
313. GONZALEZ, REV. FRANCISCO J., O.S.A., J.C.L., De Parocho Religioso Eiusque Superiore Locali.
314. HANNON, REV. JAMES J., J.C.L., Holy Viaticum.
315. SADLOWSKI, REV. ERWIN L., J.C.L., The Sacred Furnishings of Churches.
316. SEGO, REV. ARTHUR A., J.C.L., Dispensation from the Interpellations.
317. WATERHOUSE, REV. JOHN M., J.C.L., The Power of the Local Ordinary to Impose a Matrimonial Ban.
318. FREIN, REV. EUGENE B., J.C.L., The Discretionary Power of the Defender of the Matrimonial Bond.
319. CARTON, REV GEORGE A., J.C.L., The Time Factor in the Gaining of Indulgences.
320. WALSH, REV. JOHN J., C.S.Sp., J.C.L., The Jurisdiction of the Interritual Confessor in the United States and Canada.
321. UNTERKOEFLER, REV. ERNEST L., S.T.L., J.C.L., The Presiding Judge in Matrimonial Causes of First Instance.

www.ingramcontent.com/pod-product-compliance
Lightning Source LLC
LaVergne TN
LVHW050203080826
844660LV00012B/345